MW01616823

Palal

A Hebrew Teacher Explores

Prayer

A Notch in a Tent Peg

Chaim Bentorah

True Potential
REACH THE WORLD

All Scripture quotations, unless otherwise noted, are from the King James Version of the Bible.

Palal

A Hebrew Teacher Explores Prayer

Cover and Interior Page design by True Potential, Inc.

ISBN: (Paperback): 9781960024183

ISBN: (e-book): 9781960024190

LCCN: 2023943061

True Potential, Inc.

PO Box 904, Travelers Rest, SC 29690

www.truepotentialmedia.com

Produced and Printed in the United States of America.

CONTENTS

INTRODUCTION

Prayer takes on many forms. There is public prayer, private prayer, mental prayer, vocal prayer, ordinary prayer, and extraordinary prayer. You have occasional prayers and solemn prayers. Prayer comes in many shapes and sizes. Some use prepared prayers others seek to be spontaneous in their prayers. For many, prayers are mere recitations, while for others, prayer is the opportunity to pour one's heart out to God. The one common denominator of all prayer is the desire to attach or join oneself to the Almighty with the hope or desire to obtain some favor from God so as to achieve some supernatural assistance. Not to suggest that all prayer has a selfish motive. There are those who practice contemplative prayer seeking to attach or join themselves to God for just the purpose of communing with God, fulfilling that deep need to have a relationship with God.

Prayer can be summed up in the Hebrew word for prayer, which is *palal*. In its Semitic root, *palal* means a notch in a tent peg. The tent peg keeps the tent anchored to the ground, but it is that notch in the peg that holds the fabric of the tent to the notch, which keeps it anchored to the ground. Prayer is that notch that keeps us attached to God so that when the storms of life come, we will not be blown away because we are anchored and grounded in God.

I remember, as a child noticing an advertisement in a magazine for a book. The caption read that this book held the secrets to prayer. It would reveal the proper words and expressions to be used in prayer, the right form and attitude for prayer, and present a formula for prayer so that one could obtain all sorts of good things for God. Even as a child, I could not help but think: "Is God that persnickety that we must use just the right words and the right inflection in our voice to gain His attention?" Do you obtain God's favor more quickly if you pray on your knees, hands folded, and eyes closed? Is there a secret to prayer, some special formula, or some checklist to communicate with God? Do we need to hear sermons, teachings, attend seminars and classes and yes, even read books on prayer so we will know just how to relate to God and persuade Him to answer our prayer?

I remember hearing sermons on prayer where the "Our Father" or "Lord's Prayer," as we protestants call it, serves as the model for prayer. You start out first addressing whom you are speaking to, that is, "Our Father." Then you praise Him a little, you know, flatter Him, say something like "hallowed be thy name." I guess that helps put you on His good side. I suppose it will also help in the manipulation process by putting Him in a good mood so He is favorable to answer your prayer. Then you remind Him that you only want His will to be done; no matter how badly you want that prayer answered, you need to acknowledge that it is His will that must be done. Of course, you must not forget to do a little confession of sins. You can't expect God to answer prayer if there is sin in your life. After jumping through all these hoops, you are finally ready to get to the good stuff, your prayer request – "Give us this day our daily bread." That, my friends, is what prayer is all about, or so I was told.

When it comes to prayer, we tend to throw common sense right out the window. So, let's be clear on this business of communicating with God. He is a personal God who loves you and desires communication with you a million times more than you long to communicate with Him. If He is so desirous of communicating with you, He is not going to set up a series of roadblocks and barriers that you need to overcome in that communication. He has an open-door policy; just walk right in.

This is not a "how to" book on prayer. It does not reveal any secrets to prayer or special formulas. You could fill a stadium with books written on the "secrets" to prayer. Instead, this book explores the amazing dynamics of prayer, which is to achieve the primary goal of not getting all the goodies from God that you can get, but of joining yourself to God, attaching yourself to God.

There is no better way to begin a book on prayer than with prayer itself. This is not an invocation, a loyalty oath, or a prepared script, but just some dusty old professor who longs to be joined with God, attached to the God of the universe, and is simply pouring his heart out to his Creator. It is private and personal, and I only allow you to eavesdrop in this special moment between God and me when I share with God my heart as a friend would share with a friend.

"Dear Father God,

As a Christian, I was taught to address you as Lord, Father, or even as Dear Jesus. Yet your name, the name you gave to Moses, is YHWH, which, oddly enough, is grammatically feminine. So, if your name is feminine, why do I call you Father? If I call you God, that would be the Hebrew word or name of Elohim, and that is grammatically masculine. If I am referring to you as the provider, protector, and disciplinarian, then I shall call you Elohim or God, if you prefer. But if I am speaking to you as my nurturer, caregiver, and lover, I shall call you YHWH, your feminine name. Whichever name I use, you still fill me with your Shekinah glory, and that word Shekinah just happens to be grammatically feminine. Thus, to be filled with your Shekinah means that I am filled with your love, mercy, and compassion.

So, I will speak to you now in your name YHWH as you are my love, my passion, my precious friend, and my constant companion. I speak to you only with my heart and mind. For if you exist outside my heart and mind, I shall only wish to spend eternity with you. Perhaps my mind and heart exist in another realm, another dimension of space and time where I can touch you with my words. Yet, I do feel your touch and how I long for you to feel mine. In my heart, however, I know and am persuaded that you do feel my touch, for you feel my touch in these words to you.

Perhaps my mind and heart only exist in some feverish dream. I try to imagine you, your warmth, gentleness, and love. In that imagination, I am wrapped in your arms, shielded from the cares of this world as I share with you the deepest secrets of my heart that I share with no one on this earth.

You have the advantage of knowing my heart and all my inner thoughts, yet I do not know yours. Could you, for a moment, suspend the laws of nature, the laws of this physical world, so I, too, can cross those boundaries that you cross as easily as I cross through the air that I breathe? In crossing those boundaries, I shall then know your inner thoughts and heart as you know mine. Perhaps I shall find in your heart that yearning passion for love as my heart so yearns and the quest to find such love which has eluded me all my life. Does your heart long for this passionate love, this love that makes you light up with joy and happiness as mine so yearns for? If so, allow me to love you with that passionate love that none in this world has allowed me to give so that my heart might find that fullness of joy and rest in being able to express the deepest love of my heart that I have never been able to express. Perhaps to at least truly say, "I love you."

If you created me to contain such love, surely it is only a dim reflection of the love you must bear. A love you call *racham*. If I should suffer the longing to be loved, the longing to feel a gentle touch, the longing for another heart to share my heart as I should share with another's, is this not what you are? How could you have created something that you have not experienced yourself and do not understand?

You do not have a physical body, so you do not know physical pain, yet you came to earth in a human body to know what physical pain is like. You loved me so much that you wanted to know what it feels like when my human body suffers pain and torment. If you want to know what my physical pain is like, you surely want to know what the pain in my heart is like. You, too, must know what it is like to have a broken heart, to feel rejection, so when you take me in your arms, you can truly say, "I understand; I know how painful it is." As God, you did not have to feel the pain of a broken heart, yet, you chose to love, to love me who had once rejected that love. You voluntarily made yourself vulnerable, you opened your heart to me, and when you opened your heart to me, you made yourself vulnerable to have your heart broken. When I rejected your love, I broke your heart. Yet, now, when my heart breaks, I know you understand the pain of a broken heart, and you know how to best heal a broken heart.

Today a man told me I was only dreaming, that you were only an illusion and were not real. He said that you do not exist. Yet you are dearer to me than the dearest on earth, and if I should ever remove your passion and love from me, I fear I will lose my ability to breathe.

This evening as I walked up the stairs to my apartment, I felt so alone, so without love. Then at that moment, you crossed the barriers of space and time; you passed through your dimension into mine. You crossed what I could not cross; you came to me and not I to you. You came for only one reason to give me a hug so I would not feel so alone. I walked right into your arms, and I felt your hug. Oh, how I wanted to hug you back. Did you feel my hug? Please tell me you felt my hug.

In that moment, my dream of love, a passionate love that makes my heart glow with pleasure, my fantasy of being loved became real, and I knew it was your gift to me. I ask for no other gift except this one; when I am finally allowed to cross that barrier of time and space, I shall be able to look up at you and see you smile at me and see your eyes glow with pleasure. We shall then give each a hug, and you will then hold me from that moment forever. I shall then become prayer, prayer for eternity. For is that not what prayer is? Is it not simply a joining of oneself with you?

Join with me, YHWH, God, Beloved, and allow me to share your heart as I have shared mine with You. Let those who read these words discover your desire, your hope in this amazing thing that you call *palal*—prayer.

1. DESTROYING THE MYTH OF PRAYER

Do you ever stop to consider what is going on in heaven when you pray? I have shared with you a personal prayer where I have poured my heart out to God. Now I would like to share with you a dream that I believe came to me because I was meditating on this matter of prayer, I will l admit I have a difficult time remembering my dreams, so I might have added a few things to this narrative for dramatic purposes, but the basic message of my dream remains unchanged.

Last night as I went to bed, I made my request known unto the Lord. In fact, I have been faithfully making this same request for six years and have never seen an answer to that prayer. I found myself adding a little footnote to my petition that went something like this: "Well, Lord, you know I have been praying this same prayer for six years. Now I have really cleaned up my act; I have been trusting you and trying to live a good life. I would think that after all this effort, you should get around to answering this prayer."

As I slept that night, an angel appeared and declared he was my guardian angel (GA, I called him). He said my petition was up for review and that he was going to let me listen in on the discussion as to whether my petition should be granted or not. Excitedly, I followed my GA to what appeared to be a boardroom. Sitting around the room were twelve created beings, all dressed in business suits, waiting for the CEO to enter the room and begin the meeting. My GA advised me that the Owner's son was the CEO and that He was just now arriving.

Suddenly, the room lit up as the Son entered the room and took His place at the head of the boardroom table. "A suit?" I remarked, "He's dressed in a business suit?" "Hush," whispered GA; He's about to speak."

The Son opened a rather thick file and announced: "Well, our first petitioner who is up for review is this Chaim Bentorah fellow. Hmmm! Seems he has been making the same petition for six years. I suggest we check his score and see if he qualifies for an answer to his prayer. First, let's hear a report from the Human Resources department. Aleph, how has he been handling this long delay in the answer to his petition?"

An angel in a gray business suit stood up and said: "Well, he is getting a little discouraged, but he has not lost his faith or become bitter over having no answer." "Now that sure counts for something," replied the Son, who turned to an accountant-looking angel and said: "Beit, give him an A- for faithfulness. Now Gimel, how's he doing in the Public Relations Department? Any major sins to report?" A clean-faced angel with a permanent smile and a new suit stood up and said: "No change; he scores very high in that area. He does not drink, smoke, use drugs, has not committed adultery; he hasn't touched any of the big ones."

The son smiled and said: "We can always count on that category to raise his score. Beit, give him another A+ as usual. Let's look at the marketing department. Daleth, how is the soul winning coming along."

An angel in a bright white suit with a red tie and wearing an "I Like God" button stood up, shaking his head. "I am afraid we have had little progress in that department. Seems that Chaim Bentorah fellow has not used the four Spiritual Laws for over six months. He has fallen way behind in his quota of new converts." "Pity," said the Son sadly: "Beit, give him an 'F' in marketing."

"Moving now to our finance department, Vav, how's the old boy doing in his tithing?" The finance director in a gold suit stood up frowning. "No change there, boss; he has not once met 10% of his gross income." "How about 10% of his net?" asked the Son hopefully. "A couple of times," answered Vav, "but that is only on special occasions and when he was really looking for a good return. Mostly it is just spare change, and sometimes he tosses an empty envelope in the plate, just so the usher doesn't think he is some sort of Baptist cheapskate."

"Wow, that sure pulls his score down," the Son said rather harshly. "Beit, mark an 'F' for tithing. Communications department, how is his prayer life."

An angel in a sky blue suit stood up and said: "Well, it is improving; since you stuck him in that job driving a bus for the disabled, he has a lot of time between runs with nothing else to do but pray. Still, most of his prayers focus on his own needs and very little in the way of intercession. He still has that selfish streak, you know." "That he sure does," responds the Son, this time getting more annoyed. "Beit, give him a 'D.' "Teth, any better news from the education department?"

An older-looking angel in a dusty navy blue suit stood up and said: "Yes, there has been some improvement, he is spending much more time in the Word, and he is pulling in some good insights. However, I don't see him applying what he is learning too well, and I am afraid there is a lot of pride coming out as he shares his insights on his website, which is becoming more and more popular and as his books reach the bestseller list on Amazon." Now the Son is starting to get a very stern look on his face. "It's a wonder I even keep this guy on the payroll. Beit, give him a 'C.' Yod, I'm hoping you can give me something more positive from the Special Projects department.

An angel in a checkered sports coat with a lapel pin shaped like a cross flashing red, white, and blue delivered his report. "I would have to score the fellow high on his creativity. He has managed to put together a few good Hebrew classes. However, he struggles in his personal life, and his job has diverted his attention away from these. I fear he is focusing more on the here and now rather than the sweet by and by." Now the Son was really getting upset: "Beit, a 'D' and I am being merciful with that."

Wiping his brow and sitting down, the Son turns to Beit and asks that he compute the score. Handing the Son a sheet of paper, He stands to read the results. "As I read the latest performance review on this Chaim Bentorah fellow, I see he has a score of 79%. Beit, what's the minimum score for an answer to prayer?" Beit shuffles through some papers and says: "Yes, here it is; it was 90, but due to the fact that this Chaim Bentorah fellow has been having a rough go of it lately, you decided to extend some grace and lower the score to 85%." "Can we add anything for good behavior?" asks the Son. "Maybe one or two points, but not enough to put him over the top," answered Beit. "Too bad," said the Son, "I was really hoping to grant that request this time. Oh well, rules are rules." With that, the Son took a big rubber stamp and stamped my file with a red "Unanswered."

I turned to GA and sadly said, "Well, is that how it works?" GA answered, "No, that is how you think it works; let me show you how it really works." With that, GA whisks me back to my bedroom. We had stepped back in time just a few minutes to that moment when I made my request known unto the Lord. GA then turned to me and said, "This is the way it really works. You have made your request known unto the Lord; now watch what happens." I looked up, and suddenly I saw the Son embrace me with His light, and I could ever so barely hear Him say: "I'm here, it's ok, I have everything under control, just trust me and let's continue to spend some more time together."

You might read this and think how ridiculous to even imagine this is the way God handles our prayers. Yet, if you consider your struggle in prayer and trying to obtain a positive answer to that prayer, you most likely are not thinking of God's answer to your request as the outcome of a board meeting, but you have to admit that maybe sometimes you do consider the idea that God's answer to your prayer is more of a business decision than a love response.

2. THE THRONE OF GRACE

Hebrew 4:16: "Let us therefore, come boldly unto the throne of grace, that we may obtain mercy, and find grace to help in time of need.

So, what is this throne of grace that we are to approach boldly? I used to hear this verse quoted throughout my childhood on Christian radio as the station would have a time of prayer. They would begin by quoting this verse, saying: *"Let us come boldly onto the throne of grace."* I would then picture in my mind marching boldly, shoulders held high, walking with sure step up to this throne where Jesus or God the Father, or both with the Holy Spirit behind them all sitting on this magnificent chair surrounded by dozens of attending angels and presenting Him (Them) with my requests.

Of course, the first problem I have with this image is trying to picture God the Father, God the Son, and God the Holy Spirit all sitting on one throne. They are, of course, one yet in three persons as we are taught in Evangelical circles. Most preachers do a spin dance around a child's question: "When we get to heaven, will we see three individuals or one?" That nightmarish pastoral question has no real explanation that we human beings can wrap our brains around. I shall try to offer some insight into this conundrum that sends our imagination into a dizzy tailspin in later chapters of this book, but only with respect to prayer, don't expect a satisfactory explanation of the Trinity, which has eluded many Christians for centuries. Greater minds than Chaim Bentorah have pondered this question and have come up with no satisfactory response, so there is little chance this dusty old professor will offer one.

As I grew older and wiser, I began to learn that Jesus dwells within us and that our bodies are the Temple of God. So, if there is a throne room, it is in our bodies. Then again, I don't even find any mention of a throne in the Temple itself.

Going to the Aramaic, which was Paul's native language, I found that the word throne is *kursia* which is really a seat or place of honor. It is the same word used for the chairs that a bride and groom sit in when they are lifted by the celebrants during a Jewish wedding reception. The Talmud teaches that the guests at this wedding would form a circle around the bride and groom and dance. At some point during this dancing, the bride and groom are placed in chairs or *kursia* and lifted up. This is because men and women do not dance together at an orthodox Jewish wedding, but they form a separate group called a *mechitzah*. At Some point, the bride and groom are placed on a *kursia* and lifted up so they can peer over the barrier separating the men and women, and so they may see each other. The couple can connect with each other by holding either end of a handkerchief over the *mechitzah*. This is a very bold move for the bride and groom to make such a connection during the celebration before they are allowed to enter the bridal chamber and consummate their marriage. Despite the fact that this is not proper protocol, it is accepted because they are married, after all, and the whole thing takes place while everyone is dancing, rejoicing, and having fun. Herein lies the key word in our study of prayer. It is making a connection with God before we have fully consummated our marriage to Him in heaven.

This may be what the Apostle Paul is referring to about coming boldly before the throne of grace. We are allowed to break traditional protocols as the bride of Christ and make this connection between the dimensions of the natural and supernatural realm with Jesus, our groom. I believe Paul was trying to say that to approach the throne of grace is not really a somber moment but a time of rejoicing, celebrating, and dancing as one is being given the grace to become the bride of Christ. Prayer, no matter what the reason, is still a time of connecting with God, and anytime we form a connection with the God of the universe, it is a time of celebration.

The Talmud in Avoda Zara 3b talks about two metaphorical thrones that God sits upon in relation to a proselyte when a gentile wishes to enter the Jewish faith. There is the throne of judgment and the throne of mercy and grace. A proselyte was usually an idol-worshipping, non-Jew who forsook his idolatry and converted to become a Jew. A proselyte was considered born again, one who enters a new life, forsaking his pagan beliefs. He is one who is leaving idolatry to become a follower of God. But proselytes many times will convert for lesser motives than a desire to follow God. It may be a woman who just wants to marry a man who is Jewish and accepts his faith to become his bride. Just as in Christianity, many become Christians for motives other than those that centered on following God but maybe to just escape hell or get certain benefits. Such a proselyte finds God sitting on the throne of judgment. However, if the proselyte is like Ruth, who only wants to be a follower of Jehovah, then that person will enter the throne of grace, not judgment. The bride of Christ will get a glimpse of her groom and even be allowed to make a certain connection before that relationship is consummated.

The word for grace explains clearly why the protocol is allowed to be broken. You see, in the Jewish wedding, the bride and groom are married, and in just a short time, they will consummate their marriage, so why would it be so bad if they publicly connected just to glimpse each other and connect on opposite ends of a handkerchief? When we accept the grace of Jesus Christ, we are married to Him, and it is just a short time until we leave this body and consummate our marriage to Him. So, why not in this time of celebration of receiving this grace, a time of rejoicing and dancing, that we would not be allowed to catch a glimpse of the presence of our Savior?

The word bold in Aramaic is very interesting. It is *galva* (sounds like gala) and means to uncover to make, or be visible. Just as during the *mechitzah,* when the celebrants at the wedding are dancing and having fun, they will make the bride *galva*, visible to the groom, by lifting her in a *kursia*. So too, when we enter into the grace of God, we are lifted up in a *kursia* with Him so He can uncover Himself not as a judge but as a loving bridegroom filled with passion.

You see, the word grace in Aramaic is *tivota,* which is a word used among the Semitic people in ancient times and even today when one is granted entrance into a family or community. Bedouins often encamped as a family with all their brothers, sisters, cousins, and other close kin putting up their tents in a circle. Only a blood relative had access to this encampment. If someone was not a blood relative, he could not enter. Although a good friend, one who is beloved by a member of the family, may explain why this friend deserves the same rights and privileges as a blood relieve and, after a certain vetting process, could be allowed entrance into the community or encampment as he would be accepted as a family member. Still, he must be considered a member of the family. Even today in the Middle East, if someone considers a friend worthy of the privileges of being a blood relative, he will call that friend: "My brother." That is *tivota,* grace, being granted the privileges of being a blood member of a family. We are welcomed into the family of God by the Son of God, who shed His blood for us to allow us to become a member of His family through marriage.

"Let us therefore, come boldly before the throne of grace." means we have been granted the privileges of being a family member of the bride of God's Son, Jesus Christ. Prayer is our connection to His Son. Even though our marriage is not yet consummated in our Father's house, we can still connect with our bridegroom Jesus Christ and catch a glimpse of Him beyond the mechitzah of time and space.

3. GOD IS EVERYWHERE

Jeremiah 23:24: "Can any hide himself in secret places that I shall not see him? saith the LORD. Do not I fill heaven and earth? saith the LORD."

II Peter 3:8: "But, beloved, be not ignorant of this one thing, that one day [is] with the Lord as a thousand years, and a thousand years as one day."

Years ago, I was a camp director for a faith-based camp for troubled teens. In a craft activity, one of our residents built a model rocket. So, for a chapel service one day, I had our resident launch his rocket. I wrote a message to God and put it in the nose cone. The message said: "Dear God, if you get this message, kindly reply by sending a lightning bolt to destroy our staff house." The rocket was launched in a less-than-perfect launch, and there was no lightning bolt. I asked the residents why God didn't send the lightning bolt, and some answered that God would not do such a thing, but most gave the answer I was looking for, and that was that it did not go high enough to reach God. That is when I made my point that you did not have to send a message to heaven to reach God because He was no further away than your own heart.

To these street-wise kids, that did not make sense. It was a contradictory statement to them to say that God was both in heaven and in their hearts at the same time. Not only that, but He was in everyone's heart that invited Him in. Many people are like these camp residents; they just can't fathom God being everywhere at the same time. I have often heard people say: "God is too busy to know what is going on with me." Yet Scripture does teach that He is not too busy and that He does know what is going on in each of our lives. This is found in a number of passages.

19

This proved to be quite a point of discussion for the remainder of our camping session. The idea that God was not only living in your heart if you invite Him in but the fact that out of the billions in this world, you are important enough to Him that he will actually hunt you down and follow you around until you surrender your life to Him and He is not too busy with the billions of others to do it.

This apparently had a real impact on one resident. A juvenile court judge had entrusted a young teenager to our program. I remember when I received the case study on this young man. My coordinator, Ernie, was really excited because he was convinced God was going to do a great miracle for this angry fifteen-year-old youth.

I reviewed the case study and knew we were about to enter into a great tribulation period. His name was Terek. He was a member of the black underground, sent up for attempted murder, robbery, assault, battery, etc. A special note was made that he hated whites and authority. I pointed this out to my coordinator and said: "Uh, Ernie, I happen to be white and in a position of authority." Ernie ignored my concern and only spoke of the great miracle God was going to do for Terek. I had hoped that Ernie would talk about the great miracle God would do for me, like survival.

Anyways, Terek was no disappointment. When he arrived at the camp, I knew I had just met someone I had never encountered in my life. This kid just radiated hate. I looked into his eyes, and I swear I saw a real fire in those eyes. It didn't take long before the name Terek was on everybody's lips, usually preceded by a colorful adjective.

I put Terek in "Big Jim's" cottage. Big Jim was a big old bear of a guy with a fifth-degree black belt and a heart of gold. He prayed for Terek, fasted for him, loved him, and Terek repaid this love with all the hate he could muster. I knew it was wearing Big Jim down, and I remember telling Big Jim that I was going to send Terek back to the institution. Big Jim became like a momma bear who was about to see one of her cubs sent away. He told me in no uncertain terms that I would not send Terek back. He said: "Terek is me ten years ago, and I know this is his time to meet his Savior." So, I agreed to let Terek stay.

Not very long after this, Big Jim came running up to the staff house and said: "Terek is getting ready to run." I picked up the handcuffs and threw them to Big Jim, and using his hand like a ping-pong paddle, he bounced them back to me. Big Jim said: "I am not going to do it. That is just what he wants. All his life, people have told him they cared about him and loved him, and everyone has let him down. He is looking for a reason to prove I don't care, and bringing him down will give him more than enough reason. You take him down; he hates you anyways."

As much as I hated to admit it, Big Jim was right. So, I made my way down to the cottage without the handcuffs. I walked into the cottage and sat down on a bunk. Terek was the only one in the cottage and was calmly packing his bags. I remember so clearly the cold chill I felt when around him and how he had a way of just shutting out the world as if you did not exist. It suddenly occurred to me I never even heard Terek speak. Somehow, he managed to disrupt our whole program without saying a word. I tried to speak to Terek, but it was as if I was in another dimension, or maybe he was. I was certain that if I stood in the doorway, he would have tried to walk right through me as if I were just a ghostly phantom. Once his bags were packed, he calmly picked them up and walked out of the cottage. I immediately got into step right behind him.

As we walked into the woods, I said: "Terek, I don't care if you walk all the way back to Pittsburgh; I'm going to follow you. The judge put you in my custody, and that means I cannot let you out of my sight. I may have fifty other residents and a full staff to attend to, but right now, you are my focus until you return. Wherever you go, by law, I must follow you, and I cannot and will not let you out of my sight."

So, I continued to follow Terek. He took me through the woods, pulled back branches, and let them slap in my face. He took me through the swamp and the poison ivy, and after about one hour, I heard the first words I ever heard him speak: "I'm gonna go back now."

And Terek did return to the camp. I noticed something was different with Terek. The fire was gone from his eyes, and I think I actually saw fear. We sat down on a bench, and I preached my number one best sermon. He remained quiet. I was halfway into sermon number two when he said: "I ain't gonna run. Can I go back to my cottage?" Figuring my sermons were falling on deaf ears anyways, I let him return to his cottage.

About an hour later, I noticed Big Jim and Terek running up the hill to the staff house. I also noticed a strange sight. Terek was laughing and smiling. When they reached the staff house, Big Jim said: "Pic (Person In Charge), Terek has something he wants to tell you." I looked at Terek and knew what it was. Terek said: "I'm giving my life to Jesus." With that, this big, formally angry radical who was once filled with such hate, especially for whites and authority, put his arms around this big white authority and gave him a hug.

That afternoon Big Jim was taking a break, and we were sitting in the staff house talking about Terek. Big Jim asked: "What did you say to Terek?" I asked what he meant, and Big Jim said: "When Terek came back to the cottage, he was an entirely different person. For the first time, he listened to me, asked questions, and was so open to inviting Jesus into his heart that he almost begged me to pray with him. What did you say to him?" I had to admit it was not anything I said. For all I know, he did not hear a word I said. Then Big Jim asked: "How did you keep him from running?" Again, I said that I didn't; I just fell in step behind him and followed him. I mentioned that he took me through the woods, slapped branches in my face, and took me through the swamp and poison ivy. With that, Big Jim broke out laughing. He laughed so hard he almost fell off his chair. I stood there, angry. "Well, laugh will you, next time you go through the woods, get branches slapped in your face, walk through the swamp and poison ivy— I'm beginning to itch already."

Big Jim gained control of himself and asked: "Did I even tell you what made Terek so angry that he was going to run?" I replied that he had not, and so Big Jim told me: "I read the poem *The Hound of Heaven* by Francis Thompson to Terek. It is the story of a man trying to run away from God, but God followed Him everywhere He went." Big Jim then said how he told Terek in no uncertain terms: "Terek, I am praying for you, and what that means is that God is going to follow you no matter where you go until you give your life to Him. To God, there is no one else in this world, but you, and you are His entire focus."

Well, just less than an hour later, God gave Terek a nice illustration as to what that meant by having the camp director following him through the woods. As I considered God's strange sense of humor, I suddenly realized that maybe this was an illustration for me as well, to understand that God is also praying for us. If prayer is making a connection, God was surely trying to make a connection with Terek, and he succeeded, much to the suffering of his camp director. God didn't even heal my poison ivy but let it follow its natural course. I guess to reaffirm to me how He is just as anxious to connect with us as we are to connect with Him.

In theology, we call it the omnipresence of God. We can't wrap our brains around the fact that God is with us personally, every moment, every second of every day. He is totally focused on us and no one else. It is beyond our comprehension. Just like the Trinity or infinity, it is beyond our ability to comprehend. Do you ever look up at the sky at night and wonder where the universe ends? But if it ends, what would the end be like, and would that end have an end somewhere, and what would that end be like? There are things we just cannot understand. Yet, Scripture teaches that God is every-where at one time.

Jeremiah 23:24 tells us that we cannot hide from God; no matter where we go, we are never out of His sight. But there are over seven billion people in this world; could He possibly be watching every one of them 24/7? If He is talking with me, guiding me at this moment, and speaking to you and guid-ing you at the same moment, is that really possible?

I like the way it is put in Jeremiah 23:24; the Lord fills the heavens and the earth. It is like He is poured out into the universe. The word fill in Hebrew is *mele'*, which means to control, to possess, to have everything all at the same time and moment.

There are other verses to confirm this.

Job 34:2: *"For his eyes [are] upon the ways of man, and he seeth all his goings."*

Proverbs 15:3: *"The eyes of the LORD [are] in every place, beholding the evil and the good."*

Hebrews 4:13: *"Neither is there any creature that is not manifest in his sight: but all things [are] naked and opened unto the eyes of him with whom we have to do."*

Not only is He with us 24/7, He knows our every thought; we are literally naked before Him.

Is there any hint in Scripture as to how God is able to accomplish this? Maybe II Peter gives us a clue. II Peter 3:8: *"But, beloved, be not ignorant of this one thing, that one day [is] with the Lord as a thousand years, and a thousand years as one day."*

The writer seems to be quoting Psalms 90:4; *"For a thousand years in thy sight [are but] as yesterday when it is past, and [as] a watch in the night."* This is really a Semitic expression to indicate that there is no time. The prophets and Apostles all knew that for God, there is no time nor distance. In the realm of the Spirit, time does not exist. Perhaps we could better understand this point if we used the word duration rather than time. Duration is a physical thing, something that God created. God does not live in time or any duration. Einstein proved that time/duration is relative. God can manipulate time/duration any way He wishes.

Consider the fact that if God does not live in time, then the future and past are all laid out for Him. He sees what will happen in the future. Then why pray if the future is already predetermined? If He created time, He can manipulate time. He can change the future. If He can change the future, can He change the past? Would it be appropriate to pray for events that have already taken place? Logically, we could, but I have no Scripture to back that up.

There is an interesting phenomenon called the Mandela Effect. Admittedly there are many natural psychological explanations for such an event. However, it does pose an interesting observation about God living outside of time. The Mandela Effect is basically remembering something that doesn't match historical records. After Nelson Mandela died in 2013, someone wrote on social media that she distinctly remembers him dying in prison in the 1980s. That went viral as thousands of other people wrote saying they had the same memory, even down the Eulogy and flowers at his funeral. Stop and consider. Do you remember Jiffy Peanut Butter or Jif Peanut Butter? (It is Jif Peanut Butter and never has been Jiffy Peanut Butter). Did you ever watch the cartoons called Looney Toons, or was it Looney Tunes that appeared on your screen? Did Curious George have a tail? Do you remember Oscar Meyer? It has always been Oscar Mayer. Are these merely false memories, as many scientists would explain, or did some time traveler go back in time and create these changes? Could it be that God, who does not live in time, creates changes when we pray, but since history is changed, we are not aware of the change? I don't know, but if you feel led, would it hurt to pray for a past event, or is there a time when it is too late to pray? If we neglect to pray for someone's safety and they suffer because we neglected to pray, is it a done deal, and not even God can change the past? Would it hurt to pray for a past event? Could it be that Mandala did die in prison, but there were people praying for him even after he died, and God changed the past and allowed him to live many more years with great accomplishments? Of course, if the prayer was answered and God changed the past, you wouldn't know about the change unless it shows up as a Mandala Effect, a memory of Mandala dying in prison, but yet, the facts clearly say he didn't. I offer this just for your consideration as I have no Scripture to support this.

I recently read about the Large Hadron Collider (CERN) on the French-Switzerland border, where they are attempting to smash two particles together at the speed of light; they theorize that this may cause one particle to exist simultaneously in the past and the present. That they will actually punch a hole into another dimension. I mean, these are brilliant scientists, the most brilliant in the world, and they come up with these theories as scientifically possible. What was once seemingly impossible is really, in fact, possible, something existing both in the past and the present at the same time. I give to you the omnipresence of God that transcends space and time.

What we can be sure of is that God does move through time. He is not bound by time. It is like God has created our own personal universe where it is just He and us. He can be with us personally every second, every moment of every day of our lives. He can exist in your universe at the same time and be with you every moment and second of each day. Although we may each have own universe with God, we are able to interact with others in their universe and share in their universe. I am not saying this is the case, but I am only trying to illustrate how God can be a personal God. I believe it is that realization that came upon Terek and led Him to submit to God, that God was not too busy to be a part of his universe, and that scared him more than anything he faced in the streets.

Since God transcends space and time, should we pray for a past event to change? That is up to you. At least you are praying, and for that, God will be happy, even if it is impossible for Him to change the past. But, is anything too hard for God - Jeremiah 32:27?

4. JESUS PRAYS FOR US

Luke 22:31- 32: "And the Lord said, Simon, Simon, behold, Satan hath desired to have you, that he may sift you as wheat: (32) But I have prayed for thee, that thy faith fail not: and when thou art converted, strengthen thy brethren."

I mention that Jesus was praying for Terek and sent His unwilling servant to track him down. Jesus praying for us is Biblical, as we find in the above verse. Jesus prayed for Peter. This verse has always bothered me. We are always praying to Jesus and in Jesus's name, yet here is Jesus Himself who is praying on behalf of someone. To whom is He praying? Is He not God? Is He praying to Himself? Must we pray to Jesus, who then relays our prayers to God? Why did Jesus have to pray for Peter if He is God and He has all the authority and power of God?

The answer is in that word rendered as prayer. In the Greek, it is the word *edeethen* from the root word *deomai,* which means "I want you for myself." In the previous verse, Jesus declares to Peter that Satan desired to have him, and in the next verse, Jesus says: "I want you for myself." That carries the idea of making a connection, as discussed previously. However, you can't really translate it that way as the next phrase says, "that your faith does not fail." "I want you for myself that your faith does not fail" does not seem to make much sense.

In the Aramaic, the word that is used is *ba'ath* which means to be frightened or excited. *Ba'ath* expresses intense emotion. I find it hard to believe Jesus was frightened for Peter. Jesus knew all things; He knew Peter would prevail.

It would make more sense to say He was excited for Peter as he will see for himself that his faith will not fail. Yeah, it was going to be rough seas for Peter, but it will only strengthen Him. So, Jesus was saying, "Get ready, Peter, rough roads ahead, but I am really excited to watch how this will play out when you come out on top.

Then Jesus says a curious thing, "When you are converted." The word converted in Greek is *epistrepsas,* which means to return, turn from or repent. Most modern translations say when you have turned back. When he has turned back, he will strengthen his brethren. The Aramaic uses the word *pani,* which is similar to the Greek, but it is a little clearer as to what Jesus is telling Peter. We have the same word in Hebrew, and there *pani* means before, the face of, or one's presence. In Aramaic, it has the idea of turning in the sense of being released or set free.

What Jesus was telling Peter was that Satan desired to sift Peter like wheat, but Jesus said, "I want you, you're mine, but I am excited for you because this experience that will come to you will test you. It will only strengthen you so that you will be able to strengthen your brethren." The word sift, in Aramaic, is *na'ar,* which is to create a shaking to empty something out. There was coming a shaking in Peter's life by the enemy that would empty Peter of something. I am not sure what the enemy wanted to empty from Peter, but the end result was that he was emptied of all that trust in himself so that the world throughout the ages saw that his trust was in God alone. It is interesting that in the Aramaic, this is in a reflexive form so that the enemy was going to cause something to happen so that Peter would empty himself. I would guess this was the betrayal when Peter denied Jesus three times. Jesus was going to use this worst experience in Peter's life to only strengthen his faith. This harkens back to the story of Job when the enemy appeared before God to accuse Job of serving God because God paid Him so well. The enemy was seeking permission to test Job. He could not touch Job without God's permission, just as he could not touch Peter without Jesus' permission. So, the enemy was given permission as Jesus prayed for Peter.

This brings me back to this idea of praying for Peter. Why did the text not use the Greek word for prayer, which is *proseuche? Pro* has the idea of before or face to face, and *seuche* expresses the will, a wish, desire, or vow. Instead, we have the word *deomai,* which means "I want you for myself. Actually, *deomai* does express the idea of prayer because, ultimately, prayer is a joining together, and Jesus was expressing to Peter that He wanted to be joined with Peter, but Satan was going to separate him from Jesus.

The Aramaic uses the word *pani,* which means to turn to and focus your attention upon. Is that also not an expression of prayer? When Jesus said he prayed for Peter, what He was saying was that he desired to be joined with Peter and have his focus directed to Him as He has directed His focus on Peter. If prayer has the idea of joining yourself or attaching yourself to someone, then yes, God also prays for us. He also joins or attaches Himself to us when we give Him permission to do so. He is ready, willing, and longing to be joined with us; we just have to make the next move and pray or allow ourselves to be joined or attached to God.

5. A DWELLING PLACE

John 1:14: "And the Word was made flesh, and dwelt among us, (and we beheld his glory, the glory as of the only begotten of the Father,) full of grace and truth."

II Samuel 7:6: "Whereas I have not dwelt in any house since the time that I brought up the children of Israel out of Egypt, even to this day, but have walked in a tent and in a tabernacle."

The word for dwelt in Greek has the idea of pitching a tent, and it is believed that this goes back to II Samuel 7:6 and the tent of dwelling. I would tend to agree with this understanding, for as we examine this concept of the tent of dwelling in the Hebrew, we discover something quite amazing.

First, the word dwell in Hebrew is *yashab,* which means to inhabit, to set down, to abide, and is even used to be married, according to Rabbi Samson Hirsch, a 19th Century linguist, and Hebrew master. He also says that it is used to express the idea of living together and belonging. The word tent in Hebrew is *'ohel* and is distinguished from the word for tabernacle, which is *mishkan,* from the root word *shakan,* which means a dwelling place, a tent, or a resting place. Many consider the word to be synonymous, but it is really not. Rashi, the medieval Jewish commentator and Hebrew master, sees the *mishkan* as a temporary dwelling place, a friendly neighbor that is a tabernacle which was a portable dwelling place from God. The *'ohel* was a dwelling place within the *mishkan,* or as Rashi explains, that *'ohel* was a curtain that set off a room in the *mishkan.* In other words, the *'ohel yashab* was the Holy of Holies which was the resting place for the Ark of the Covenant, where the presence of God dwelled.

31

The Ark of the Covenant was lost during the time of Jesus; there was no Ark in the Holy of Holies in the temple, just the stone the Ark rested upon. But John was saying that God dwelled in Jesus just as he dwelled in the Ark. That is curious because, as discussed in the previous chapter, does not the Bible say that God dwells everywhere in the universe, Psalms 139:8, Proverbs 15:3, Matthew 18:20, and Jeremiah 23:24?

Jesus was like a living Ark of the Covenant. The very presence of God dwelled in Him in a special dwelling like a home. God may dwell everywhere in the universe, but He could not make everywhere His home. He could not dwell in darkness as He is light. The world was filled with darkness, and he needed a vehicle that was cleansed and pure to move into darkness.

When John said that the Word was made flesh, he was referring to Jesus, and when he said that Jesus dwelt among us and we beheld his glory, he was making a reference to the Ark of the Covenant in the Holy of Holies, which was a dwelling place or the home of God. That was in the Tabernacle or the *mishkan*. The place where one prepared to enter the *shakan* of God, which was the Holy of Holies that was His home. The Jewish Talmud and Midrash have a very interesting explanation for this.

The Jewish people, as the chosen people of God, were to be cleansed continually through the rituals performed in the Tabernacle or temple so that their bodies could be a home or dwelling place for God. Does not Paul tell us in II Corinthians 6:19: *"What? know ye not that your body is the temple of the Holy Ghost which is in you, which ye have of God, and ye are not your own?"* The Apostle Paul seemed to suggest that this idea of our bodies being the temple of God was common knowledge among the Jewish people. Their mission was to bring the light of God into the world just as we, as believers, are to bring the light of God into the world after the blood of Jesus Christ has cleansed all our sins and made it possible for our bodies to be a pure dwelling place for God, a temple, a home for God. Our mission on this earth is to be a home or a *yashab* dwelling place for God, just as Jesus demonstrated by being the Light of the world who bore the very presence of God in His human body. That is not to say we are divine like Jesus, for He was God incarnate. We, in our bodies, merely provide a home, a *yashab*, a dwelling place for God, the Holy Spirit, and Jesus Christ to live in. We are His Light bearers, not the Light Himself.

Let's take a closer look at the Ark of the Covenant. The Ark was a box that rested in the Holy of Holies in the Tabernacle. It contained the two stone tablets of the Ten Commandments, a Torah scroll, Aaron's rod that budded, and a vessel filled with manna. It was really three boxes in one. The outer box was made of pure gold, the center box was made of acacia wood, and the inner box made of gold. The Talmud teaches that this instructs us that our outer man and inner man are to be pure gold. The Ark was said to have weighed around a ton. When it was transported, it was covered with a veil made of skins and purple cloth to be hidden from the eyes of everyone, even the priest. It was to be carried by staves or poles that passed through the sides of the Ark. Unlike some of the phony pictures you see about the Ark, it had no feet but rested directly on the ground. The poles were to never be removed, and only the priests from the line of Kehot could carry the Ark. It was forbidden to be transported by a wagon that was pulled by an animal. There was a *kaporet*, or golden cover, that covered the outer box, and on top of the cover sat two *keruvim* or cherubs that faced each other with their wings towering above the Ark.

The Ark's home was the Holy of Holies, the most sacred chamber in the Tabernacle and later the temple. It rested directly on the *Even Hashetiyah* – the *Shetiya* stone, which, according to the Talmud Yoma 54b, is believed to be the foundation point of the entire world. This was said to be the stone that Jacob laid his head upon as a pillow when he had the dream of the angels ascending and descending on a ladder or staircase. Only once a year could the High Priest enter this chamber which was on Yom Kippur, to perform the annual service before the Ark. This was the time of the most intense worship of God.

When King Solomon constructed the first Temple, he built an alcove deep within the Temple Mount to conceal the Ark. Realizing the threat of the destruction of the temple during King Josiah's reign; he hid the Ark in this alcove according to II Chronicles 35. However, the Talmud argues that the Ark was actually sent to Babylon in Yoma 53b. Today, it is now the most sought-after ancient archeological artifact.

In the Midrash Yalkut Shimoni Shmuel II 5:142, it is taught that the Ark actually carried its carriers. When the Kehot priest lifted the Ark to transport it, instead of them carrying the Ark, the Ark literally carried them. This was to demonstrate to the nation that it was God who was carrying Israel to the Promised Land, to battle, and to their eternal home. This is why a wagon was not to carry the Ark, for God was not carrying a wagon home but his people. That is also why an animal like oxen or mules could not pull a wagon, for God did not need the strength of animals or man to transport His presence. In other words, there was something very supernatural about this Ark.

Here is the thing that is very interesting. The Talmud and Midrash discuss some unusual features or characteristics of the Ark, which suggest that it is really a "ghost" artifact. I would offer this for your consideration only. You see, according to the Talmud, the space occupied by the Ark did not take up space. The Holy of Holies was ten cubits wide. According to the Torah, the Ark stood in the center of the Holy of Holies with a length of two and a half cubits. Yet, when measuring from the sides of the Ark to the wall, it was five cubits on each side. If you had five cubits for each side of the Ark, that measures ten cubits, the entire length of the Holy of Holies. So, where do you put the two-and-a-half cubits for the Ark? According to the Talmud in Yoma 21a, Megillah 10b, and Bava Batra 99a, the Ark was taking up space but was not taking up space. It was sort of a ghost. It occupied space in heaven and earth at the same time.

So, what is this special presence of God? Well, let me offer this thought. I was reading something that is believed by what some call mystical Jews. They are called mystical because they believe you can have a personal relationship with God, a one-to-one communication with God. Apparently, that makes them mystical. By that definition, many of us Christians are just as mystical as the mystical Jews. These mystical Jews teach something called *tzim tzum*, or presence through absence. This is complicated, and I am going to try to put it into very simplistic terms, so forgive me if my explanation falls short of the full intent. God cannot dwell where there is darkness. Darkness rules this earth. So, He can only dwell in a state of purity and sinlessness. That is why our bodies are the temple of God. Jesus Christ, through His shed blood, cleanses us of all our sin and darkness so God can dwell through us in the special relationship, that special presence like the presence around the Ark. Like the south pole of a magnet is attracted to the North Pole so too is the believer who is cleansed by the blood of Jesus attracted to God. However, if sin dwells within a person, then it is like the North Pole being repelled by the magnet's south pole. We can feel the presence of God, but we cannot be joined to God if there is sin in our lives. When that sin is confessed, and we are cleansed, then we enter that special presence of being joined to God.

Now here is the thing about *tzim tzum*. *Tzim Tzum* is like the Ark of the Covenant that did not dwell in space and time yet, was still present here on Earth—presence through absence. So too, when we worship God, we are taken into the realm of God, but only if we are pure in heart through the blood of Jesus. Otherwise, we are just standing on the outside of the Ark and looking at a piece of furniture. There are times in our worship, because of the cleansing blood of Jesus, that God brings us into such a pure state that we can actually enter that *tzim tzum*, just as Jesus in a fleshly body was able to be in the realm of heaven and earth at the same time as witnessed by the disciples at the mount of transfiguration. We are presently not in the *tzim tzum* state like Jesus was, but we are permitted to touch the Ark, the special presence of God. That is why Uzzah died when he touched the Ark, for the Ark was in a state of impurity being carried by a wagon powered by an ox, and that made anyone coming in contact with the Ark ritualistically impure. In other words, he tried to enter that *tzim tzum* in an impure state. When our bodies are continually being purified by the blood of Jesus Christ, we are able to enter in and out of the realm of heaven, dwell in that *tzim tzum*, that bubble that exists in both heaven and earth, the natural and supernatural at the same time and truly enter into His gates with thanksgiving Psalm 100:4.

Jesus *shakan* or dwelled on this earth as the true embodiment of the Ark of the Covenant. Thomas was instructed and/or permitted to touch the body of the resurrected Jesus, that body that was in *tzim tzum*, and unlike Uzzah, he was not struck dead for the blood of Jesus removed any ceremonial impurities so that we can *shakan* with Jesus Himself and He can *shakan* in our bodies.

6. FAITH AND PRAYER

Genesis 15:6: "And he (Abraham) believed the Lord and He counted it as righteousness."

Exodus 19:17: "And Moses brought forth the people out of the camp to meet with God; and they stood at the nether part of the mount."

Matthew 17:19-21 Then came the disciples to Jesus apart, and said, Why could not we cast him out? (20) And Jesus said unto them, Because of your unbelief: for verily I say unto you, If ye have faith as a grain of mustard seed, ye shall say unto this mountain, Remove hence to yonder place; and it shall remove; and nothing shall be impossible unto you. (21) Howbeit this kind goeth not out but by prayer and fasting."

So, if prayer is a connection, what can we say about that connection, and how does it relate to the word in Hebrew for prayer, which is the word *palal,* and what is the connection to faith?

The Talmud teaches that *trusting belief* in God is more important than anything else. One may keep all the laws of Torah and follow every ritual, but it is only trust that will ultimately save the individual. Remember how Saul lost his kingdom? He performed a sacrifice before a battle rather than wait for Samuel to arrive to do it. Samuel was late, Saul's army was deserting him, but Saul would not go to war until that sacrifice was offered, so he did it himself. What was his sin? Yes, disobedience as the sacrifice had to be offered only by a consecrated priest. But I never heard a Christian preacher or teacher give the root reason. I had to go to Jewish literature to find it. What is taught by many Jewish teachers is that the reason Saul lost his kingdom was that he was not trusting or believing in God. Ironic that we, as Christians who know and understand that our salvation is in faith in God alone and not works, will not see this, yet the Jews, whom we say depend upon works, are the ones who do recognize faith as their cornerstone, go figure.

The Talmud teaches that if a drowning man suddenly spots a tree within reach, which part of the tree does he lunge for? Not the branches, for they will break under his weight; rather, he grabs the roots of the tree. Trusting in God is similar to the strong roots of a tree; it is the basis and foundation of the entire tree, our salvation.

The word in Genesis 15:6 for *believe* is *amen*. Does that sound familiar? You use it every time you end a prayer and usually without thinking as to why you end your prayer with "amen." When you trace this word to its Semitic roots, you find that it has its origins in the nursing of a baby. Consider the dynamics involved in a nursing baby. The mother must cradle the baby in her arms. The baby is in total protection of its mother. The mother is providing sustenance to the baby directly from herself, not from a spoon or cup, and it is her own milk, not the milk of a goat or cow. The impressionist artist Mary Cassatt in her famous painting entitled *Louise Nursing Her Child* depicts a mother nursing her child with the mother looking at her baby with total love in her eyes and the baby looking up to its mother with total trust and dependence in its eyes. That painting could easily have been named *Amen*. Mary Cassatt spoke volumes in this painting, portraying the deep bonding taking place between the mother and child. This is why I use the word *trust* for *amen* rather than belief, although our English word *belief* does fit *amen*.

As a man watches his wife nurse their baby, he is seeing a picture. In this picture, she is fulfilling her role as a helpmeet, for she is giving this man a visual demonstration of belief, amen. From this, he can begin to understand what *amen (trust, belief)* in God really means. Yet, a man cannot understand the full meaning of *amen*, at least not like a woman, for he cannot feel or experience *amen* like a woman. That is why it is so important for a woman to learn to love her husband like she automatically loves her child so she can be an *'ezer kenegedo, helpmeet* to her husband, a gateway to understanding the love and nurturing of God.

I remember hearing the wife of a veteran who was badly burned in combat. His face was totally disfigured, and he refused to believe that his wife could still love him. The wife said she had to learn to love him as she would a child before it was born, and then as she nursed him back to health, this veteran began to realize that he had to learn to amen—believe that his wife really loved him before he could fully recover.

It is interesting that the Bible uses the Hebrew words *'ezer kenegedo—helper who stands before him* for the word *helpmeet*. The enemy knows how dangerous a woman is to his cause. Through the granting of the ability to bring life into this world and experience the intimacy of nursing that new life, she has been given knowledge of the love of God, and she has been assigned the duty to pass that knowledge on to a man. No wonder the enemy is creating pornography and sexual perversions and is out to destroy the home. Therein lays the very core of understanding the love of God. Is it any wonder that the enemy wants to promote the male as a dominant role rather than just a leadership role? He has to keep the woman underfoot lest she reveals the true nature of the love of God to her husband. It was never intended by God for a woman to be dominated by her husband; he was only to be a leader. The woman was created to *'ezer kenegedo*, to stand before the man and be a gateway to the knowledge of God's love.

That is why Solomon said in Proverbs 18:22 that whosoever finds a wife finds a *good (tov)* thing. I really dislike the use of the English word *thing* in this passage. That is obviously a male translation. I like the Living Bible's rendering; "Whosoever finds a wife finds a treasure." The word *tov* means to bring into harmony; thus, whosoever finds a wife finds a treasure, someone who can bring him into *tov—perfect harmony* with God.

Regarding this matter of faith, I have pondered Matthew 17:19-20 for many years. The disciples came to Jesus asking why they could not cast the demons out of the boy that Jesus was able to cast out. Jesus said because of their unbelief. Some translations render Jesus's words as saying they had so little faith; the NLT says they did not have enough faith. Countless books have been written as to how we can have more faith. If someone isn't healed or prosperous, it is because they did not have enough faith. This not-enough faith business seems to be Christianity's favorite excuse as to why our prayers are not answered. Thus, there are sermons, podcasts, books, teachings, and whole organizations built on developing your faith. Teachings on how to exercise your faith like you exercise your body. The more you exercise, the stronger you become. The more you exercise your faith, the stronger it becomes. People are desperate to have more faith because they believe the odds of getting an answer to prayer are much better if you have gobs of faith rather than a *little* faith.

I have heard sermon after sermon that the whole problem with Christianity is that Christians have so little faith. Yet, Jesus follows up this declaration of *little faith* by saying all you need is the faith of a mustard seed, and you can move mountains. Some gift shops in Israel made a fortune gathering little seeds of mustard and putting them in a little crystal-type ball the size of a pearl, attaching a chain to it, and making it into a neckless so one who visited Israel could return to impress all the people back home by saying: "Lookie here, this is a mustard seed and all you need is faith the size of that seed." The question that always comes to my mind, and surely yours as well, is: "How do you measure something so subjective as faith with something so objective like a seed?" What constitutes little faith as opposed to big faith or whole gobs of faith?

I ran across something interesting as I studied the works of Jewish teachers throughout the ages. They often make a reference to *paradatha' dacharadal,* which is the Aramaic for a grain of mustard. It is not a reference to a mustard seed but a mustard grain. A seed is used to grow a mustard plant or bush, but a grain is harvested and used for food. Thus, the emphasis is not on the size but on its use. The word grain in Aramaic is *parad* in its root form, which means grains as a noun, but as a verb, it is used to separate and/or scatter. In one place in the Talmud, I read that a *paradatha' dacharadal* was used ceremonially in the cleansing of a circle of priests. In other places in Jewish literature, I found the grain of mustard was a purifying agent. A grain of mustard is not eaten directly as it has a very sharp taste but is used as a seasoning. Even our Western product called mustard is used to season a hot dog or hamburger to give it a sharper taste. I even found in the Mishnah that the mustard grain is forbidden during Passover because it causes bread to leaven.

To most of us in the Western world, when we think of mustard, we think of hotdogs, bratwurst, and hamburgers. But to the mind of the first century, they had no concept of hotdogs, bratwurst, or hamburgers. What was a grain of mustard to them? As a Biblical language teacher, with the help of a younger brother who is a linguist, I tried to put what I read in Jewish teachings regarding mustard grains or seeds into a context of the first-century

Middle East and what the disciples heard when Jesus said that if they had the faith of a grain of mustard, they could move mountains.

In Exodus 19:17, we learn that the people of God assembled at the foot or base of Mt. Sinai to receive the law. But wait, it does not say in the Hebrew that they stood at the foot or base of Mt. Sinai; it says they stood *bethchethith beneath or underneath it*. This comes from the root word *tavach*, which means underneath. Of course, no Christian translator worth his Ph.D. is going to translate that as standing *beneath* or *underneath* the mountain. I mean, God would literally have to pick the mountain up and hold it over the people. That is ridiculous, almost as ridiculous as having the faith of a grain of mustard seed and telling a mountain to be cast into the sea—Matthew 17:20. Actually, in the Babylonian Talmud 88a, the Jewish sages do teach that God literally picked up Mt. Sinai and dangled it over the heads of the people. This was likely a bedtime story told by every Jewish mother in the first century. I wonder if Jesus could have been making a reference to this event. This account in the Talmud teaches that God actually picked up Mt. Sinai and held it over the heads of the people as they declared their faith to follow the Torah or the law, and thus with that faith, they were able to command the mountain to be removed from over their heads. Of course, it is ridiculous to think that two thousand years later, the Messiah would reference this crazy event under Mt. Sinai by saying in Mark 11:23:

> *For verily I say unto you, That whosoever shall say unto this mountain, Be thou removed, and be thou cast into the sea; and shall not doubt in his heart, but shall believe that those things which he saith shall come to pass; he shall have whatsoever he saith.*

Or again in Matthew 17:20:

> *And Jesus said unto them, Because of your unbelief: for verily I say unto you, If ye have faith as a grain of mustard seed, ye shall say unto this mountain, Remove hence to yonder place; and it shall remove; and nothing shall be impossible unto you.*

Surely Jesus was only giving an illustration. He could not have been referring to a real event. Or could He? You explain to me why the writer used the word *tavach underneath* and not the word *yalad*, which means at the foot of or beside. The ancient sages and rabbis don't try to explain it away like we Christians of little faith try to do. For you see, little faith may not mean what we traditionally believe it means.

Let's say that God actually dangled a mountain over the heads of his people to get them to ratify the law. I mean, isn't that coercion? That is literally saying, "Ok, you've got faith as the grain of mustard seed right now, but you had better use it, or I will drop this mountain, and the nation will be nothing but a grease spot." That would be like threatening someone with hell and saying, "Well, you have enough faith to believe in hell; how about using that faith as a grain of mustard seed that sparks a belief in hell to accept Jesus as your personal Savior?" In other words, using fear, threatening people with hell to get them saved. I daresay, however, that there are many who have entered into salvation and a relationship with God through a powerful fire and brimstone sermon.

The Talmud teaches that God had to put His people into a fearful situation to exercise their faith at this early stage of their development as a nation of God. One thousand years later, we find in Esther 9:27:

> The Jews ordained, and took upon them, and upon their seed, and upon all such as joined themselves unto them, so as it should not fail, that they would keep these two days according to their writing, and according to their [appointed] time every year.

The Talmud interprets this as the Jews reaffirming their divine law and the faith they exercised to accept it when it was first established but now, not out of fear as when their faith was immature and young, but out of love for God. Just as someone accepting Jesus because they are afraid of going to hell will, they will one day mature to accepting their relationship with God out of love and not fear of going to hell. Here is where we come close to what I believe Jesus was teaching about a grain of mustard seed.

In the Aramaic, Jesus did not say it was their lack of faith or no faith, but it was a *lashaimanutha,* which could mean no faith, but as used in Jewish literature, it is often rendered as an impure faith. It would then make sense for Jesus to use the grain of mustard as an illustration, for in the mind of the disciples of the first century, they would be thinking not of the size of their faith but of the purity of their faith. Now this was a big deal for the Jews as it is today and should be for Christians.

Consider Matthew 14:30-31:

> *But when he saw the wind boisterous, he was afraid; and beginning to sink, he cried, saying, Lord, save me. (31) And immediately Jesus stretched forth [his] hand, and caught him, and said unto him, O thou of little faith, wherefore didst thou doubt?*

Here we have the story of Peter, who jumps over the side of a boat and walks out to Jesus on the water. He must have gotten close enough to Jesus before he started to sink, as all Jesus had to do was reach out and grab him. I mean, that is not a "little" faith; that is whole bunches of faith. Yet, poor Peter is scolded for having little faith? When Jesus lifted him out of the water, his faith must have been restored, as we don't read about him sinking again.

So why was Jesus scolding them with, "Oh, you of little faith." I mean, it sounds as if Jesus is absolutely disgusted with them. But who says Jesus was scolding them? In Greek, that exclamation "oh" is not found in the text; it is simply "You of little faith." The word little, in Greek, is *oligos,* which means small in number or quality. The preposition "of" is not there either and could be rendered as "You have little faith" or "You have a little faith." The Aramaic is a bit more clear. The word for little is *zeora* with no exclamation "oh." Church tradition sticks that "Oh" in there, which has no business being there except that the translator and the church which sponsored the translators wanted it to be there to provide good sermon material on how we need to build our faith and why miracles do not happen. It is simply, we have little faith, shame on us.

Zeora could mean little, but that is misleading for this word. The word really has the idea of someone who is young and inexperienced. It is used for an apprentice who has not yet mastered a certain skill. Literally, Jesus is making a statement to Peter; it is in a simple Piel form. "Your faith is yet quite young." The implication is: "Why are you afraid? You have faith, it is young and inexperienced, but you do have faith. Peter, you are inexperienced in faith, but dog gone it, you have faith, why doubt?" Remember what it says in *I John 4:18: "There is no fear in love, but perfect love casteth out fear: because fear hath torment. He that feareth is not made perfect in love."* Once the love of God, God's *racham* love, is perfected in us, our motivations will be based on love and not fear of hell or some punishment.

Little faith is also a reference to faith that is not yet pure. The disciples had faith, gobs of faith, whole bunches of faith. But Jesus said they could not cast out the demons because they did not have pure faith. Their faith was immature, inexperienced, and filled with a lot of selfish thought. Maybe they wanted to impress people with their supernatural power; maybe they just wanted to experience power. There can be many selfish personal desires mixed in with your desire to serve God. It makes for *lashaimanutha* impure faith. Pure faith is faith that has no hidden agendas, faith that has no distortion. It is a faith that believes in the pure truth of God, that He is a God who loves, cares, nourishes, and through the redemption of His Son Jesus Christ, who lives inside of us. It is a faith that is not dependent upon reason, just a total trust in the love of God that He has your back. You are not alone; you have been bought and purchased by a price, the blood of His Son Jesus, and as His personal, precious possession, He is hanging onto you tightly.

Pure faith in prayer is prayer where you are not playing games with God. Would you pray, "God give me a brand new, candy apple red Tesla so I can drive little children to Sunday School on Sunday morning? Maybe you are planning on driving little children to Sunday School in your brand new Tesla, but odds are that it is just a little game you are playing with God to win His favor to grant your request. Your real motive is to own and drive a brand-new car. That is what you call *lashaimanutha*, impure faith, faith that is filled with ulterior and/or selfish motives.

How do we get this pure faith? Jesus told us in verse 21: *"Howbeit this kind goeth not out but by prayer and fasting."* Prayer in both Hebrew and Aramaic is *palal,* and as explained earlier in its Semitic root, it refers to the notch in a tent peg. Prayer is what secures us to God, so when the storms of life come, we are not blown away. Pure faith is attaching yourself securely to God. This comes through fasting, which is denying your physical body of its demands. In fasting, you take your eyes off yourself and focus your full attention on God. When that happens, you have no agenda but the agenda of God's heart. No motives but the motives of God's heart, and when securely attached to God, you have a certainty of His lovingkindness and caring protection. In a word, you will have pure faith. Pure faith does not come from clinching your fist and repeating over and over: "I believe, I believe." Prayer is attaching yourself to God and focusing your full attention on Him in pure faith.

7. THE TABERNACLE, A SYMBOL OF OUR HUMAN BODIES

Ex 25:3-8: "And this [is] the offering which ye shall take of them; gold, and silver, and brass, And blue, and purple, and scarlet, and fine linen, and goats'[hair], And rams' skins dyed red, and badgers' skins, and shittim wood, Oil for the light, spices for anointing oil, and for sweet incense, Onyx stones, and stones to be set in the ephod, and in the breastplate. And let them make me a sanctuary; that I may dwell among them."

God asked the children of Israel to build a tabernacle to be a sanctuary. Actually, the word sanctuary is *mekodash,* meaning *from a separate or holy place.* In other words, a special place. This did not mean that God did not dwell anywhere else but in the Tabernacle. He indeed encompassed the entire earth and universe. But the Tabernacle and/or temple was to be a special dwelling place. I think we all have a special place we go to meet God when we pray. Sure, God is with us 24/7, and we are constantly calling upon God throughout the day, but there is also a need for a special, special place, like a portal where we go to read His Word and pray and commune with Him.

Our Christian tradition renders the word *betokam* as *among,* from the words, *"that I may dwell among them."* Yet, we Christians totally ignore the preposition before *takam,* the Beth with means *in.* We get the suffix right which is the pronoun *them,* but according to Jewish teaching, the word really is rendered *within them.* We Christians arrogantly teach that God only dwelled in Christians after Jesus returned to heaven, which is not the teaching of Judaism. God always dwelled in the hearts of the righteous. Grace always abounded. God does not live in time. The past, present, and future are all the same to Him. People in the Old Testament were saved just like today; we trust in the finished work of a redeemer, a Messiah whom we say is Jesus Christ. We in the natural world, the world where time exists, look back to the finished work of Jesus Christ, the people of the Old Testament just looked forward to the redemptive work of the Messiah. Paul says: *"Know you not that your bodies are the temple of God."* I Corinthians 6:19. That phrase *know you not,* is a rhetorical question; it has an obvious answer that everyone should automatically know. If this was a new concept to the Jews, it would not be rhetorical. Rabbi Menachem Mendel Schneerson, a highly respected Orthodox rabbi, is quoted as saying that the sanctuary or tabernacle is a model and prototype for all subsequent homes for God, i.e., our bodies.

Thus, the Tabernacle is a picture of our human bodies. Hence Scripture places an overwhelming emphasis on the construction of the Tabernacle as opposed to the implementation of the Tabernacle. From the very beginning of the Tabernacle in Exodus 25, everyone was to give an offering or contribution to the construction of the Tabernacle because it represented the human being, and everyone was pictured in the Tabernacle. Every item placed within the Tabernacle had some function, from the table to hold the shewbread to the candlesticks to carry a flame. The only item that had no function whatsoever was the ark of the covenant. It had one purpose, and that was to carry the presence of God. There were three crowns in the Tabernacle. One for the Altar where the High Priest performed the sacrifices, the table which held the shewbread, which provided bread for King David and was a crown for royalty, and the Ark of the Covenant, which carried the presence of God and was ultimately for everyone. The Ark had two poles which were never to be removed to indicate that the Ark was to always be portable, ready to carry the presence of God wherever man was. Just as we are to carry the presence of God to the world no matter where we go. The Ark was to be made of gold on the inside and outside to show that the presence of God was not only inside of us but was to also reflect our outside that which the world would see.

Thus, if the Tabernacle, or *mishkan* as it is known in Hebrew, was a picture of the human body as Paul describes. Then what did the fifteen materials used to build the Tabernacle represent? The answer to that is found in the Jewish commentary called the Midrash HaGadol (the great study). These 15 materials were all donated and correspond to the human being as follows:

1. Gold – The soul of the human being

2. Silver – The body of the human being

3. Copper – The voice of the human being

4. Blue – The human veins

5. Purple – The human flesh

6. Red – The blood of the human

7. Flax – The intestines of the human

8. Goat hair – Human hair

9. Ram skins dyed red – The skin of the human face when flushed by God's presence.

10. Tachash – Human skin color.

11. Acadian wood – Human bones

12. Oil for lighting – Human eyes

13. Spices for anointing – Human nose and mouth

14. White stones - Human kidneys (center of one's life force)

15. Gemstones – The human heart.

The one item you may not recognize is the *tachash* which is just a transliteration because Christians have no translation for it. Your Christian lexicons will say *tachash* is a badger but admit that really it is an unknown animal that is likely extinct. Jewish tradition teaches that it is a multi-colored animal solely for the purpose of sacrificing its skin for the Tabernacle. The color of this animal encompassed the skin tones of every race of human beings to show that all races of man with every skin tone were loved by God equally.

You see, the Tabernacle was created not as a monument to God but to man's relationship with God. It was all to represent that man's redemption would come through one who took the form of man, which we believe is Jesus Christ, the Messiah who was the Son of God, God incarnated who took on human flesh and form, who walked this earth, who suffered as we suffer in a dying body. He would one day come to redeem us from this dying body leaving only a spirit totally cleansed and purified to become one with God. When this dying body finally breathes its last and releases its spirit, it will be joined permanently with God. That is why the Ark of the Covenant was to be built using half cubits, i.e., 4.5 length, 1.5 width, and 2.5 height. This is to show that our journey here on earth to become one with God can only be met halfway as we are encumbered by a physical body that is decaying. In God's timing and God's plan, when He brings that body to its natural end, our spirit will then be free to add that final .5 and become one with God. The Bible does teach, however, that there will be a resurrection. Thus, our spirit, joined with the Spirit of God, will enter a new physical body that is like that of Adam and Eve before the fall, incorruptible and eternal.

Everything in the Tabernacle was to be constructed precisely as God commanded because our human bodies were created exactly as God intended them to be created. Some vessels for honorable use, some for dishonorable use but all according to God's divine plan and purpose.

This presents to us one of the basic dynamics of prayer. When we pray, we are not sending out prayers into outer space, to some celestial city floating out there like some starship with a throne room and a large throne where God Himself sits and captures all these words directed to Him from this little blue marble called Earth. When you pray, you are joining your heart with the heart of God Himself, Who dwells within you. Your words go no further than to what is dwelling within you. God created an elaborate tabernacle, later a temple, in order to give a physical picture of His dwelling place and where we are to direct our prayers.

So, what do we do with verses like II Chronicles 7:14:

> *If My people who are called by My name will humble themselves, and pray and seek My face, and turn from their wicked ways, then I will hear from heaven, and will forgive their sin and heal their land.*

Clearly, that verse teaches that God will hear us from heaven. The word heaven in Hebrew is *hashamayim* which is in a plural form. Hence, I will hear from the heavens. The word hear is *shama'*, which means to hear, respond, obey, and/or answer. The context indicates that when there is a famine, if God's people will humble themselves and pray and seek His face, God will answer from the heavens, i.e., send rain. He is not hearing you from heaven, He only answers from the heavens, but His listening takes place in your heart where He dwells.

8. THERE ARE NO IMPURE PRAYERS

Leviticus 4:7: "And the priest shall put some of the blood upon the horns of the altar of sweet incense before the LORD, which is in the tabernacle of the congregation; and shall pour all the blood of the bullock at the bottom of the altar of the burnt offering, which is at the door of the tabernacle of the congregation."

I read something very interesting recently in the Talmud in the Mishnah of the Order of Mo'ed. There were two altars in the Tabernacle and later the Temple. One was the copper altar, or the brazen altar, where the animal sacrifice took place, and the other, near the Ark of the Covenant, was the golden altar, or the altar of incense.

Everything in the Tabernacle, the vessels, the fabrics, the tools, and even the clothing worn by the priest could become and did become impure and had to go through a cleansing process. As the Tabernacle and Temple were to be a dwelling place for God, they had to be totally pure, holy, that is, sanctified. Everything except two items, the brazen altar and the golden altar. These two items would never become ritually impure.

The Tabernacle, or the *mishkan* as it is known in Hebrew, was a picture of the human body. All materials and items had some relationship to the human being, as indicated in the last chapter. Our bodies are the temple of God and a dwelling place for God. But God cannot dwell in our bodies any more than he could dwell in the *mishkan* if there were impurities present.

It is the blood of the sacrifice that makes the impurities pure. But that is not all; there must be prayer. The Hebrew word prayer, *palal*, speaks of making

49

a connection with God. The Bible tells us that without repentance, there is no forgiveness of sin Acts 3:19. The brazen altar was where the blood was shed, and the altar of incense represented the prayers of the people, which included their repentance. Both altars were needed for the redemption of sin and the purification of the *mishkan.*

The brazen altar that is within us is the sacrifice of Jesus Christ and the shedding of His blood. The altar of incense would be our prayers. Both bring about purity, so logically, the instruments creating purity cannot become impure.

Just as anything in the *mishkan* can become impure and must go through a process of purification, so too, anything in our bodies can become impure; our minds, our hearts, our eyes, our feet, our ears, etc. are all subject to impurities. We need the brazen altar to be purified, and that is Jesus Christ, who was the sacrifice for our sins. He cannot become impure as he is the means to our purity. But there is something else that dwells within us, and that is the altar of incense, which are our prayers, through which we can repent and thus be attached to Jesus Christ, whose blood will make us pure.

What this is saying is that even like Jesus, who will never be impure, our prayers can never be impure. Just as the brazen altar and altar of incense can never be impure, all our prayers to God are pure.

In James 4:3, we learn: *"Ye ask, and receive not, because ye ask amiss, that ye may consume it upon your lusts."* This does not say we receive not because we pray impure prayers; it just says we pray amiss. The word amiss in Aramaic is the word *bisha',* which means to be wrong or incorrect. We ask wrongly because we are asking according to our own desires or lusts. Still, we are not condemned in this verse for praying even though they are lustful, selfish prayers. It is only saying that we do not receive a positive answer when we pray according to our lust. The word lust in Aramaic is *ragag,* which means desires, but desires that make you anxious or restless. That is a prayer uttered without giving much thought as to whether what you are asking for is right or wrong; it just seems to be the thing you need at that moment to make everything correct.

If you lose your job, the first thing you think of is to find another job, and you immediately pray: "Lord, give me another job." I remember when I lost a job, and my first prayer was for another job immediately. However, I did not receive an immediate job. At the time, I thought that was the right thing to pray for. But my father had a stroke, and I realize now the loss of that job gave me time to be with him and encourage him. I had prayed wrongly because I was frightened, anxious, and worried about how I was going to pay the bills. God helped me to manage that while I was able to spend some time with my father. My prayer for a job was not impure; it was just based on a selfish desire, not according to God's will.

I remember years ago; I heard a woman give a testimony as to how she was saved. She left her home as a teenager and ran off to Hollywood, seeking to become a movie or television star. That never happened. She went through the Hollywood scene, married, had a child, and divorced, all the while struggling to break into the film industry. As a single mother, she had to work as a waitress and other low-level jobs to support her child and herself while still trying to make it big in the entertainment field. Then one day, her child became ill, and the doctor told her it was a serious illness and her child would likely die. That was the straw that broke the proverbial camel's back. She got into her car and drove out into the desert, where no one was around for miles. She stopped her car, and for half an hour, she screamed out to God every obscenity and vulgar word she knew. She cursed God and Jesus, and she said that if she knew there was a Holy Spirit, she would have cursed him also. After a half hour of cursing God out, she sat back, exhausted. In the strange silence that usually follows a lot of screaming, she heard a gentle, loving voice say: "That is the first time you have spoken to me. I love you." She broke down, repented, and surrendered her life to Jesus, and all that impurities were covered by the blood of Jesus.

She reached out to God in prayer, and of course, no prayer is ever impure to God.

9. A SANCTUARY

Psalms 73:17: "Until I went into the sanctuary of God. Then understood I their end." (A psalm of Asaph)

Most people believe that worship only takes place in a church and in a sanctuary. Many feel their prayers will get a better hearing from God if prayed in a church sanctuary. I remember holding a Hebrew class for a number of inner-city pastors, and the host pastor explained that the only room available during the time our class was to meet was the sanctuary. When my team and I entered the empty sanctuary, one old boy came running up to us and told us to remove our hats. When he learned we were holding a Hebrew class, he immediately went to the host pastor to express his disapproval of using the sanctuary for something other than worship and prayer. To him, there was something sacred and holy about the sanctuary, and to use it for something other than preaching, singing, and prayer was very disrespectful. We felt somewhat in agreement and held our class in the pastor's office.

We know little about the man Asaph. We are not sure if there were many different Asaphs mentioned in the Bible or if such a person named Asaph even existed. Many Bible scholars feel it was just a pen name. Some believe the name represents a group of people. Commentators generally agree that the Asaph, who wrote the Psalm in our study verse, was a close friend of King David and collaborated with him on much of his poetry and music. This Asaph was also a seer. The Bible does show a difference between a *seer* (ra'ah) and a *prophet* (nebim). Simply stated, people would go to consult with a seer, but a prophet would go to consult with the people. If this Asaph was a Levite who functioned in the role of a seer, he would have had many people come to him for counsel as people would go to their pastor or priest today. As a seer, like many pastors today, Asaph saw the sufferings and anguish of God's people, and he could not help but contrast this with the prosperity and problem-free life of the wicked. In Psalm 73, Asaph is only repeating the question that he was most likely asked by the many who came to him for counsel. That question would be: "I have served God, sacrificed for Him, lived for him, worshipped Him, and yet I am suffering. God has made many promises, but it seems like He has not kept them. Why?" On top of that, there is the issue expressed in verse 13: "I have cleansed my heart in vain." In other words, what good is there in serving and worshipping God, in receiving a pure heart, if you get nothing in return?

Indeed, the world is filled with a lot of gold diggers who accept Jesus as their Savior, hoping to get all sorts of goodies. I remember a famous preacher was being interviewed on secular television. The host asked the question: "So you mean to tell me that if you accept Jesus as your Savior, He will solve all your relationship problems, financial problems, and health problem? If you are in a wheelchair or have terminal cancer, all you have to do is accept Jesus as your Savior, and you are healed. I mean, who would not want to accept Jesus? I would accept Him if I would get all that." The preacher totally missed the point and just jumped up and said: "Well, let's just pray right now!" The talk show host only shook his head. What he was saying is that what this preacher was teaching is that God is some sort of celestial genie in a bottle. Prayer is no more than rubbing a magic lamp and poof! You get your wish.

Indeed, I have found many Christians who worship only with the intention of receiving something in return. Many Christians will bounce from church to church in search of a church where they can *feel the presence of God.* I was listening this afternoon to a pastor being interviewed on Christian television who said his church was named the Presence of the Lord Church, and if there was ever a Sunday when anyone did not feel the presence of the Lord, they would change their name. No doubt, there were many who came and left the church because they did not feel the presence of God. The presence of God is not dependent upon a geographical location or a preacher's relationship with God. It depends upon the individual.

True, there are special moves of the Spirit of God, like during Pentecost and revivals. However, Jesus reminds us in John 3:8: *"The wind bloweth where it listeth, and thou hearest the sound thereof, but canst not tell whence it cometh, and whither it goeth: so is every one that is born of the Spirit."* These moves of the Spirit of God and His presence are at the will of the Holy Spirit and not some human effort like playing certain worship music, clapping your hands, or dancing and singing. This will not bring the presence of God.

We treat the presence of God in church like we are attending some séance where we try to conjure Him up with loud music, hand clapping, dancing, and singing, as you find in many pagan rituals. If someone doesn't feel the presence of God, they call it a *dead church.* There is something of a selfish motive that rings in such a statement. They are worshipping God to get their personal needs met. They desperately want something from God, a healing, a financial miracle, or just to have a good time and be entertained. They want a lively, joyful worship service where they can feel the presence of God, and if they can get God in such a good mood, He will more than likely grant their requests.

I have heard a number of people comment that they tried Christianity, but it just does not work. What they are saying is that they bought into all the hype of Christianity that God will solve all their problems, restore their marriages, relationships, and finances, and then when they accept Him, things seem to only get worse. These people are really saying like Asaph: "I have cleansed my heart in vain." In other words, "I spend all this time worshipping God, and nothing ever happens." Well, I hear you; most of the time, nothing happens for me either. There are many worship services I leave not feeling refreshed or joyful. I grew up on the old hymns and gospel music. Most modern churches today play contemporary music, which I personally detest. Not that it is bad or sinful; it is just not my cup of tea. It all sounds the same and just drones on and on while I make desperate attempts to praise God. The music doesn't draw me into worship; it hinders me from worshipping. I find myself longing for one or two of the old hymns or choruses I used to sing as a child. I know that I will surely feel the presence of God if we would just sing one verse of *Love Lifted Me.* Yet, I know if they did play "my" type of music and I felt uplifted and euphoric, that would not necessarily be the presence of God but my own emotions being aroused by pleasant memories. I discovered as I grew in my relationship with God that I could really worship Him and feel His presence no matter what music they played. For His presence does not depend upon whether or not I like the music.

Still again, during my worship, I prayed for healing, but I just got worse. I prayed for restoration, but things were just too far gone to be restored. I mean, I can keep you up all night telling you about my unanswered prayers. So why do I bother trying to live a good Christian life? I get no personal benefit from not cheating on my taxes. Sometimes I stop paying my tithe because I just can't afford it, or I just get downright plain selfish. Either way, I am no less blessed or no more blessed. But is that why I pray, *palal*, attaching myself to God, to get the good things in life?

I recall one time a prosperity teacher came to the church I was attending when I was working a secular job. Oh, he gave all these testimonies or case studies of how people who started to give extra offerings to a building fund like our church was trying to do and how God blessed them. He then had people stand up and pledge in front of everyone what they were going to give, and then he collected a special offering for the building fund. Then he told the pastor to be sure and allow the people to share testimonies the following Sunday on how God not only gave them back the money they gave but increased it tenfold. I was a rebel and refused to give a dime. That week, to my great surprise, I got a promotion at work with not only an increase in salary but a $2,500 bonus. My first thought was: "Why didn't I throw a few bucks in the kitty?" Then I would be giving a wonderful testimony on how God blessed me. Oh, the amens I would have received, the compliments people would have given me. I would have been a hero. But you know what? That is not what I signed on with God for. I signed on for better or for worse, for richer or for poorer, in sickness and in health.

This matter of why the righteous should suffer and the wicked get a pass on suffering is an age-old question that usually goes unanswered. Even today, it seems the wicked are prospering in politics. They are getting their atheistic agendas granted while we poor Christians are losing our freedoms every day; we are being censored and mocked by the media while the Christian voice is silenced. I listen to prophets predict that in a few months, yea, a matter of weeks, the government will issue indictments, and all these wicked people will go to jail, yea and even the government will change, and we will have a God-fearing person as our President. Yet, it never happens.

When I start getting such attitudes, I have to be like Asaph. It is time to go into the sanctuary to discover an answer to all these questions. Asaph went into the *sanctuary*. Is this sanctuary a church, an auditorium, a sacred place? It could be. It could also be my one-bedroom apartment, or for someone incarcerated; it could be a prison cell.

Sanctuary in the Hebrew is a mysterious word. It is *mikodeshi,* which is literally: *my place of separation or my place of holiness.* The Masoretes ended the word with a *Sere Yod,* which would give it a plural ending, and thus it would be an allusion to the Holy of Holies. Some say it is in the plural because there are three divisions to the sanctuary: the court, the holy place, and the Holy of Holies. However, I question this as Asaph was not a high priest and could not have entered the Holy of Holies. As a seer, however, he would have a *holy place* or *separate place* that he would have entered to receive his revelations from God. Perhaps as a priest, he could have approached the Holy of Holies. Still, I would take issue with the Masoretes, and as many rabbis do, I would end the word with a *Chireq Yod,* which would create the pronoun *my.* This is important because it shows that when Asaph needed an answer from God, even as a seer, he had a *special place, a quiet place* where he would go to pray and worship God.

We have times of worship when we are with other believers in a church sanctuary. We have times of worship when we gather for a home Bible study. Families have their family altar where they worship God as a family. Then there are those quiet times, those times when you are alone like I am now, and it is just you and God, and you have a personal time of worship and prayer with God.

It is in this special *quiet place,* this *mikodeshi,* that God reveals His secrets to us. It is here He can have our full attention. It was here that Asaph found the answer to that age-old question of why the righteous should suffer when it seems like the wicked are always prosperous and winning.

Many translators render the last word in this verse, *'achar* as *end.* However, its primary meaning is *after, behind,* or *to tarry.* Stretch the meaning, and you can get *end.* *"Then understood I their end."* If we say *end,* then that suggests that in this *quiet place,* what Asaph saw was the *end of the lives of the wicked,* which is in everlasting torment. The righteous, however, will end up in heaven after a life of suffering. In other words, the translators wanted to answer the question of why the righteous suffer and the wicked prosper in the word *achar.* This is to say that "it will all pan out in the end."

However, let's just stay with the general meaning of *achar*, which is *to tarry* and not try to stretch it to fit our agenda or personal bias. If we say tarry, then what Asaph would have been saying is that in this quiet place, this sanctuary, he understood why the wicked *continue* or *tarried* in prosperity. What Asaph came to understand is that as he worshipped in the presence of God, he felt, in his quiet place, that peace and joy in the presence of God, which answered the question for him. Let the world have its wealth, prosperity, its comfortable office chairs. For when you enter into worship with God and feel His presence, then everything else means absolutely nothing. When you experience the presence of God, you are aware of His eternality. All the struggles of this world, the fears, and the problems dim in the light of eternity. More often than not, the answers to our prayers are not direct answers but simply God reminding us that what we are seeking is temporal, but our real need is eternal, and His presence covers a lot of our temporal needs. Until we enter our *quiet place* or *mikodeshi* and begin a personal time of worship, we feel our greatest needs are temporal, but in our sanctuary, we discover our true needs are eternal. There is an old hymn that teaches us to turn our eyes upon Jesus, and the things of this world will grow strangely dim.

I recently received an email newsletter from a Christian organization and read yet another story of a Christian who was shot to death in the Middle East. The only crime this Christian committed was to love Jesus and try to share that love with others, and for that, he was murdered. Like Asaph, I went to my *mikodeshi, my quiet place, my sanctuary*, where I sought an answer from God as to why He did not save this faithful servant, the one who lost his life in the Middle East. As sometimes happens in my *mikodeshi, my quiet place*, I find I fall into a time of worship where I enter the heart of God, and when I did, He let me feel what this Christian felt when that terrorist pointed his gun at this Christian's head. It was like I was looking into the face of Jesus, and all I felt was peace, serenity, and joy. I felt the longing to reach out and hug Jesus and believing at any moment; my arms would be around Him and His around me. When I left my sanctuary, I felt such a letdown that I almost wept. I actually began to feel depressed that I did not get to hug Jesus physically. I had to return to my world, my life, and my problems without being able to hug Jesus in His world. My instant thought about that Christian martyr was, "You lucky child of God." That is when I understood the last words of Psalms 73:17 *"Then understood I their end (or continuing)."* I sensed God saying, "I will be there when you need Me. Just enter that time of worship as I draw you into My heart. *Palal,* attach yourself to me." I knew and understood that those who seemingly prosper when we who are faithful get the short end of the stick; they do not have what we have. Our ace in the hole is the very living, loving life of Jesus Christ, and because of His finished work on the Cross, we can worship Him anytime; we can attach ourselves to Him anytime and anywhere, for our bodies are the temple of God, our bodies are that sanctuary of God, and it goes with us wherever we go. That Christian who died at the hands of terrorist rebels was in the sanctuary, caught up in worship, in the arms of Jesus. He received a Divine Kiss just as wonderful as if he were raptured out of this world. He knew and understood that God is there whenever we need Him. We don't need to run to a church or sanctuary, for He exists within us. Nothing this world has to offer can come close to that. God will be there when we need Him. Our comfort will not come from our jobs, bank accounts, or anything this old crazy world has to offer. We can't depend upon any of that. But we have something no one can take away from us; that is the sanctuary in our hearts where we can, at any time, enter into praise and worship.

10. PRAYER SUPPORT

Proverbs 21:9: "[It is] better to dwell in a corner of the housetop, than with a contentious woman in a wide house."

Up until now, I have been addressing prayer as something personal. I believe Scripture teaches that prayer is a family adventure as well. I would use Proverbs 21:9 as my text for this theory.

I have always been bothered by this verse, well, not so much the verse but the preachers and teachers who mention this verse. Generally, these preachers and teachers are male and bring it up to elicit a laugh which usually comes from the men and a few good-natured women.

Whenever I heard this verse, even as a child, I could not help but wonder why it was the women who got the bum rap. All the women I knew in my life as a child, mother, grandmothers, aunts, and cousins were never brawling or contentious to my observation. Besides, after walking this earth now for these many years, I've met plenty of men who could be just as brawling and contentious as any woman. Having been a pastor and involved in some pastoral counseling, I often found that if a woman was contentious, it was usually the husband's fault for neglecting her. Many times, I didn't blame the woman for being contentious; she deserved better treatment and attention than she was getting.

The other thing that bothers me about this verse is that the wisest man who ever lived advises a husband to cower in a corner when his wife goes on a rampage. That does not sound like very wise advice to me, nor something that the God I love would recommend.

There are alternatives to translating this verse that fit more of God's style. Let me give you one that I like. The verse started off with "It is better." The word here in Hebrew is *tov* which means good but also means to be in harmony. It is more in harmony for a man to dwell in the corner of a housetop. For one thing, the preposition is not "in" but 'al, which means to be above, among, or beside. The word corner is *panah,* which in its Semitic root is a word used for a bulwark, tower, battlement, or *support.* I like the word support. It is more in harmony for a man to support his wife in a battlement *gag.* The word *gag* comes from the root word *ga'al.* Sure, it means a roof or housetop which is supported by a *panah.* There is, however, a double meaning here that the Hebrews would easily pick up that we in the 21st Century would not. The Hebrews were more familiar with this word as being used in the Tabernacle for the Altar of Incense. The Altar of Incense was where one would burn incense to pray intercessory prayers, that is, to offer prayer support for another. Perhaps there is the idea of seeking shelter, but this is seeking the shelter of intercessory prayer to support one's wife in prayer. But this is also good advice for a woman whose husband gets argumentative or contentious. So why is the woman singled out?

The word contentious or brawling is *midinim* which is also a word used for someone who is very *competitive; he* or she just cannot stand to lose in any encounter. Here is why the woman is being singled out, as a man is considered the leader of the household; although equal with his wife, you still need someone who is in charge. I believe this verse is saying that if the wife is in disagreement, it is better not to enter into an argument but for the husband to support his wife's feelings and concerns and go into intercessory prayer over the situation. He is to be the leader or example of prayer in the house.

There is one other thing that is very interesting. The text uses the word *chavar.* Many translations render this as a *wide* house; some translations just ignore this word. But this word is just too juicy to ignore. It is a word used in the Garden of Eden in reference to the serpent, who was called the *chavar* or the enchanter. You know, there are some men who just love their wives so much that they can't say no to them. They will give them everything they want, trying to please them, and the wife plays on this being that seductive little kitten, maybe giving a little pout, turning her head away, and the old boy gives in against his better judgment. She has him eating out of her hand; she has *chavar* or enchanted him.

I believe this verse is pointing the finger at men just as much as women. Both should be careful, and both should seek the *gag*, the Altar of Incense, intercessory prayer, and it should be the man who leads the prayer before entering into any fight or using powers of manipulation. In other words, as prayer is the joining of oneself to God, it is also meant to a joining of a husband, wife, and God together. A husband and wife who pray together will together join or attach themselves to God.

Prayer even goes beyond a family exercise. In Acts 2:42, we learn: *"And they devoted themselves in the apostle's doctrine and fellowship and in breaking of bread, and in prayers."* Fellowship with a community of believers is also a joining and attaching oneself with others and with God.

Luke, who wrote the Book of Acts, was an extremely educated person. He was of Greek origin and educated in the Hellenistic city of Antioch. He studied Greek philosophy, medicine, and art. Tradition holds he made paintings of Peter and Paul and was the founder of Christian iconography. So, what amazes me about Acts 2:42 is that someone who is so steeped in the Greek culture and Greek language would write this verse in a very Aramaic style. In Greek, as in English, we would write this passage as "And they devoted themselves in the apostle's doctrine, fellowship, breaking of bread and in prayers." The Greek and English would not repeat the word "and." We just stick a comma after each word in a series and stick the "and" at the end. In the Aramaic, as in the Hebrew, you use an "and" or a conjunction after each word in a series, as Luke does here. Luke could very well have written the Book of Acts in Aramaic as he was addressing an Aramaic-speaking audience.

The word for fellowship in Hebrew is *asephah*, and in the Aramaic, it is *shauteph*. Both words are agricultural words used for the swarming of insects that would devour a crop. Insects swarm for protection. When the Nile River in the Middle East overflowed, it would kill off a single fire ant. However, in times of flood, thousands of fire ants link themselves together to form a raft. By doing this, they would not drown as they would if they tried to navigate those waters on their own. I believe that is why the Aramaic Bible, the Peshitta, uses the word *shauteph* for fellowship.

Throughout the history of the Jewish people, *shauteph* was their means of survival. When troubles came, they would link up with each other, young and old, married and single, women and men, and share each other's burden, like those fire ants. They formed one massive family, and together, they were able to survive throughout a history of persecution. When persecution came, all doctrinal or theological differences became mute, they were all Jews and united as one family.

Many Christians today are questioning why they should go to church. They listen to music that they really do not like and hear sermons that they have heard all their lives. They go through a door, sit down, get a little show, get up, and leave. Churches, in order to maintain their congregations, seek to provide music that would attract the most people, they seek to give sermons that would appeal to a wide audience, and they may have small group activities such as women-only or men-only Bible studies, children programs, singles only programs and teenage programs. Again, you come and go and never really develop an overall sense of community.

But if persecution or trouble arises, these separate little bands will discover their real reason for coming together; they will *shauteph,* join hands, link up with each other, young and old, male and female, singles and married, and form one large life raft so that no one person would flounder. It is then that they will discover what real fellowship means. They will not come together because they like certain music, play softball, or have a potluck dinner; they will come together to survive, and the one ingredient that brings them together is their mutual love for Jesus.

I drove a woman in my disability bus to her church the other day, where she met with a few other ladies to put together little toys for the children in their church to play with during the service. As we talked, I learned she was a real born-again Christian who loved Jesus with all her heart. She then bemoaned the fact that her church was a mainline liberal church, and her pastor did not even believe the Bible was inspired and questioned the deity of Jesus. Like the good Baptist that I am, I asked her why she did not join a Bible-believing church. She then said that she had many friends in this church who also loved Jesus, and when her husband passed away, the church came together for her, supported her, and helped her through that difficult time. She said: "I could never leave them." Her faith in God is firm, but what she really needs is *shauteph,* which she has found.

Just as a husband and wife are joined together with God when they pray together, so too does a community of believers join themselves together with God when they pray together. There are times when prayer is personal practice with God; then there are times it is family practice with God, and other times it is a community practice which brings all in unity with God, joining or attaching to God. Yet, when times of trouble come, God does not expect us to stand alone. He has given us the ability of those fire ants to join or link ourselves together through prayer and create a raft to help us navigate the storms of life.

11. STANDING IN THE GAP

Deuteronomy 31:6: "Be strong and of a good courage, fear not, nor be afraid of them: for the LORD thy God, he it is that doth go with thee; he will not fail thee, nor forsake thee."

This last chapter leads us into the teaching of intercessory prayer. How powerful is intercessory prayer? On a national level and even global level, when there is a major crisis, there is a call for prayer. This would be a call for intercessory prayer.

I heard a news commentator say that never in his forty years of journalism has he heard more serious talk about the threat of a nuclear war. This came during the war in Ukraine, where initially, every expert in foreign affairs was saying that nuclear weapons would never be used in the war. Yet, after a few months of war, there was serious discussion as to the amount of destruction and the casualties that would result from a nuclear exchange. Some were even saying it was not *if* nuclear weapons would be used but *when* and how do we prepare.

A few weeks ago, as I was driving my disability bus through downtown Chicago, I heard a series of popping sounds like gunshots going off, and suddenly I saw cars picking up speed. I cannot be sure if they were gunshots, but shootings and murders have been on the rise in the city. I had one passenger beg me not to take the expressway to downtown Chicago because there were so many reports of drive-by shootings on the Eisenhower Expressway in the news.

Whenever we enter an election year, there is always one political party pounding one major theme, and that is that the opposing party is responsible for the rising crime rate, and unless you elect representatives from their party, there will be anarchy and chaos taking over our streets, even worse than at present.

Our nation went through a pandemic, and you couldn't sneeze or cough without people looking at you like you had leprosy. Even though the government assures us we are living in a post-pandemic period, we still see people wearing a mask, fearful they will get a virus and die.

One cannot help but wonder if the enemy has not released his all-powerful and most effective weapon on us, and that is fear. So, how do we handle this fear? How do we go about our lives without that constant black cloud hanging over our heads? Maybe I sound old fashioned, but I do not live in that fear because I believe the Word of God to be true and dependable, and when God says: *"Be strong and of a good courage, fear not, nor be afraid of them: for the LORD thy God, he it is that doth go with thee; he will not fail thee, nor forsake thee."* I personally believe that if God tells me in His Word that I have nothing to fear when I am in His care, then like some naïve child when his father tells him not to be afraid, I will not be afraid.

It doesn't matter whether you are Jewish, Catholic, Mormon, Baptist, or even a Muslim; if you acknowledge God Jehovah as your only God and you depend upon Him and submit to Him and are learning to love Him as your only God, you are under his umbrella of protection, and you have nothing to fear. I realize that being so inclusive can be offensive to some of my readers, so I will pause to let you find some good rocks to stone me with. But when God says that if you repent and turn to Him, He will hear you and respond. He does not give a checklist of theological dogma to follow; just repent and submit to Him.

Note how God first admonishes us to be strong or *chazaq* in Hebrew. *Chazaq* has the idea of being firm. This is better understood as focused. If we are focused on God and His love for us, we have taken our first step to overcome fear. Then He tells us to be of good courage. Note the word good is *tov*, which is to be in harmony or, in this context, in harmony with God. The word courage is *'amatz*, which is being obstinate. That goes along with focus. It is being firm in your focus on God and not letting the latest news reports distract you from your attention on the God who loves you. Then we are told to fear not. That word for fear is *yara'* in Hebrew, which really means to honor, respect, and stand in awe. We are not to stand in awe of the power of nuclear war. We are not to honor the terror of criminal and murderous activity in our cities. We are not to respect the threat of a pandemic. All that the enemy uses to create fear in us should not be respected, honored, or cause us to stand in awe of its power. We are then encouraged to not be afraid. We may think fear and being afraid are the same, but they are two different words in Hebrew. The word for afraid is *'arats*. Now that is the word we apply our English word fear to in the sense of concern for our own safety. Here is where it gets a little controversial. We are told to look out for number one, one being us or me, myself and I. I recall a student I had who served in the military in special forces and fought in combat. I asked about fear, and he said, of course, he felt fear, but only when he was alone. When he was with his team, his focus was on his teammates and their welfare, watching their backs. In those situations, he had no incapacitating fear. He felt anxious, aware of the danger to himself, but his concern for his teammates, not letting them down, and watching their backs caused what fear he had to heighten his senses and draw upon his training and skills. In other words, what fear he felt only made him more effective in caring for his teammates. The fear that causes you to cower and hide, the fear that causes you to stick your head in the ground, does not exist when you are seeking the welfare of someone other than yourself.

Then we are told that the reason we can overcome fear is that God goes with us. More precisely, it is *YHWH Eloheka*, the Lord your God, who goes with you. Earlier, I spoke of *YHWH* being in a feminine form and speaking of the feminine nature of God, that loving, caring, merciful nature of God. *Eloheka* is in a masculine form and speaks of the masculine nature of God, that is, the disciplinary, provisional, and protection of God. It is sort of like when I was a child, and I was in the hospital. My mother came to visit me, and I felt comforted; then, I remember a few minutes later, my father entered the room, and when he entered, I felt protected. It is both the loving and protective nature of God that goes with us.

More than that, He says that He will never leave us. The word leave in Hebrew is *yarepeka* from the root word *yaphah,* which actually means to be weak. However, it is in a Hiphal form that is causative, and in the context of forsaken, it means that God will not cause you to be weakened because he will not forsake you.

Deuteronomy 31:6 provides the formula for freedom from fear. We are to just focus our entire attention on God and His lovingkindness for us, we must not let anything distract us from that focus on Him, and if we do that, we will recognize that He is both our comfort and protector, and He will not allow us to become weak by forsaking us.

Can we even find comfort in the threat of nuclear war? Note Isaiah 40:15: *"Behold, the nations are as a drop of a bucket, and are counted as the small dust of the balance: behold, he taketh up the isles as a very little thing."* In the Hebrew, this is literally saying the nations are as a drop *on* a bucket. It adds nothing to the weight of a bucket filled with water. It is like spitting in the ocean; it is of little consequence. Putin and his 5,799 nuclear warheads are inconsequential to God. A simple utterance from Him and every one of those warheads can be activated or deactivated.

Let me take you just three verses earlier to Deuteronomy 31:3: *"The LORD thy God, he will go over before thee, and he will destroy these nations from before thee, and thou shalt possess them: and Joshua, he shall go over before thee, as the LORD hath said."* Note that God says: *"He will destroy the nations before them."* In some passages that speak of Israel going to battle, the word *charam* is used, which is a destruction involving a separation; in that context, it is just to separate his people from evil. In this verse, the word for destroy is *shamad,* which is an annihilation to remove any threat. It is God who removes the threat. Even if it is a nation with 5,799 nuclear warheads, it is nothing for God to annihilate the entire nation before any threat.

I read that there is some speculation that the reason Putin said nothing about nuclear weapons after the first time he made the threat was that when he made the first threat, he ordered all his nuclear warheads on alert. This article mentioned that we know the United States and Israel together developed a computer worm that infiltrated Iran's nuclear centrifuge, almost causing a catastrophe when they started it up. The article suggested that it wouldn't take a much greater effort to develop a similar worm into the systems of Russia's nuclear warheads, and when they went to put their warheads on alert status, it took some quick technological thinking to prevent the warheads from arming themselves and triggering a nuclear explosion before the missiles even left the silos, destroying the entire nation. Hence Putin pulled back his threat until they could get rid of the computer worm. Would it take too much for God to release a little virus into the nuclear system which would end up annihilating the whole country before they could launch?

The point is, God is in control of the nuclear forces of this world. He is in control of every pandemic, every criminal justice system. He could interfere anytime He wants to. He can interfere with free will when his people, like with Moses, stand in the gap for their nation. Then God has to interfere with man's free will to launch a nuclear attack to honor the prayers of His people. Israel was moving toward self-destruction in Exodus 34 until Moses interceded, and then God said, "Ok, for your sake, I will interfere with man's free will as it is the only way I can answer your prayer. Moses, stood in the gap for an entire nation, and as a result, that one man standing in intercession was all God needed to prevent the destruction of an entire nation.

My point is that we have nothing to fear from nuclear war because the power to prevent it lies with believers who are willing to stand in the gap. Ezekiel 22:30: *"And I sought for a man among them, that should make up the hedge, and stand in the gap before me for the land, that I should not destroy it: but I found none."*

Even if God chooses to bring this world to an end, we have nothing more to fear than Moses, who said in Deuteronomy 31:2: *"And he said unto them, I am a hundred and twenty years old this day; I can no more go out and come in: also the LORD hath said unto me, Thou shalt not go over this Jordan.* He spoke these words on the day that he was to die. He knew that within 24 hours, he would be dead. We think that when he said: "I can no more go out and come in," he was saying he was so weak he could not move. Yet, look at Deuteronomy 34:7: *"Moses was a hundred and twenty years old when he died, yet his eyes were not weak nor his strength gone."* NIV Moses was still strong and vigorous, he had plenty of strength, but his mission on earth was completed, and God was going to just take him home. He knew he was living his last 24 hours, and he used that time to speak his heart to the people he loved to encourage them to continue to serve God. He was not afraid to die, for his focus was not on himself but on God and the people he loved. In fact, he was at total peace with his passing. Another more important reason was that he saw his brother Aaron pass, and he prayed for the same death as his brother—to receive the Divine Kiss.

I spoke of a Divine Kiss in an earlier chapter. It is what the Jews call a passing without any suffering or agony, without fear, only absolute peace. For the Christian who has completed their earthly mission, it is everything you would expect with a rapture. Christians believe that if they live when the rapture occurs, they will not suffer death, that their bodies will be changed instantly to heavenly bodies, and they will be caught up to be with the God they love. The Divine Kiss is really no different, except you just leave your body, but you will get a new body eventually. However, you leave your body just the same way as a rapture, with no fear, no agony, no pain, just closing your eyes and opening them again in the presence of the God you love.

For me, rapture or Divine Kiss, there is no difference. You get removed from this world of pain and disappointments with no terror, no fear, no suffering, or agony. Just one moment and all is changed for something greater than we can imagine. When I hear of wars, rumors of wars, disasters, pandemics, or crime, all I think about is the words of Rusty Goodman, who wrote a song after he was diagnosed with terminal cancer and had just a few months left on this planet "Lately, All I've Been Getting, is Leavin' On My Mind."

In this day of fear, intercessory prayer is one of the most powerful spiritual gifts that God has given us. There is not one of us who cannot enter into intercession for another or for a nation. The power of your intercession is only limited by your desire and your passion to intercede. In intercessory prayer, we focus on others, and when we focus on others, like that student I had who was in special forces, his personal fear was muted.

12. WHY GOD LISTENS TO OUR PRAYERS

Exodus 19:5: Now therefore if you will obey my voice indeed and keep my commandments, Then, you will be a peculiar treasure unto me above all the people, for all the earth is mine."

Why does God listen to our prayers? Because we are a peculiar treasure to Him. So, all we have to do is obey God's voice and keep His commandments, and we become His peculiar treasure. I love the idea of becoming God's treasure, but that peculiar business doesn't sound good. When I think of treasure, I immediately picture an old pirate's chest filled with gold and valuable gems. Even though being a peculiar treasure sounds good, I really want to know more specifically what that relationship with God really is. We need to examine just what a peculiar treasure really is to understand why God is so interested in our prayers.

The word *peculiar* is not in the Biblical text. It was just a little paraphrasing by the translators of the KJV for the word *segal,* which they say means a peculiar treasure. Most modern translations will more correctly say a *treasured possession.* That word for *peculiar treasure segal* really has the idea of being a possession. It is used for something that is highly prized. We will be a special possession to God. The letter Samek in the word indicates that this possession is one which is carefully protected and sheltered. The letter Gimel indicates that this is a prized, beloved possession, and the final letter, Lamed shows that this is a possession that he keeps developing and upgrading. As His peculiar treasure, we are under His protection, we are beloved and prized, and he keeps polishing us and upgrading us.

The numerical value for *segal* is 93. The numerical value of the Hebrew word for inheritance or heirloom is also 93. I drove a 93-year-old woman to the dentist on my disability bus today. She lives alone and said she was robbed twice in the same month. The thieves stole items that belonged to her grandfather, a pocket watch, an old comb, and a pocket knife. The insurance company could only give her a few dollars for these items as that is all they were really worth, but to her, they were priceless. Sometimes we look in the mirror, and what looks back at us doesn't look like anything of value. We are nothing but a handful of dust. Some people may be poor, unknown, unaccomplished, or uneducated, but if they obey the voice of God and his commands, they are like that pocket watch, old comb, or pocket knife was to that elderly woman. A treasured heirloom may be worthless to everyone else, but it was a precious possession to her, as we are to God. So precious to God, in fact, that His own Son died on the Cross for that seemingly worthless lump of clay.

Maybe in the eyes of the world, you feel you are worthless and of no interest or value to anyone. But God promises that if you obey his Word and seek His voice, you will be more valuable to Him that an NFL $100 million dollar talent superstar football player. If that football player does not harken unto God, God will consider him just another of the 6 billion people that he created and loves that do not listen to or obey His voice. Yet, this seemingly unknown, worthless lump of clay that has harkened to the voice of God will get His full attention and become prized as a precious possession.

What does it mean to harken or obey the voice of God? The word voice is *qol* and means to express a thought either out loud or in some manner to another person. How many people hear a voice or God's thoughts out loud? He did speak out loud on Mt. Sinai and when Jesus was baptized in Matthew 17:5, but how many of us actually hear the audible voice of God? Yet, He has given us His Word, the Scriptures, which also express His thoughts. Hence to read His Word is to hear His very thoughts, but we must read and study His Word to know His thoughts, and in doing so, we know what to obey.

We are the children of God. Parents will make great sacrifices for their children, and if their children harken to their voice, they will learn to follow the right path to a full and successful life. I just read about a young woman who grew up in poverty. Her single mother made only $15,000 a year. They lived in a trailer house which sometimes had electricity and sometimes did not; it all depended upon whether there was enough money to pay the electric bill. The woman loved her mother and listened to her instructions. She also observed how her mother would sacrifice so many things for her sake and to help her get an education. Her mother would sometimes go without food herself to make sure her daughter – her *segal*—her peculiar treasure, had enough to eat. Her daughter, now grown and successful, credits her mother's dedication to the happy and fulfilled life she is now living. Her mother can only delight in the satisfaction that she contributed to making her daughter happy. Would not our Divine Father find great delight in the same way?

For many parents, there is nothing they would not do for their child. God gave us earthly parents as a natural illustration of His love for us, and the fact that He would not hesitate to sacrifice anything for us, even to give His own Son, shows how much of a treasure we are.

God listens to our prayers because we are His children, His *segal*, His peculiar treasure.

13. SILENT PRAYER

Ephesians 6:18: *"Praying always with all prayer and supplication in the Spirit, and watching thereunto with all perseverance and supplication for all saints."*

That is a curious statement: "Praying always with all prayer and supplication." Paul uses the Aramaic words *kal tsalun*— all prayer. *Kal* means all, the whole ball of wax, everything, prayers of thanksgiving, intercession, petitions, group prayer, personal prayer, fervent prayer, etc. Then Paul says supplication in addition to all prayer. Some translations say petitions or requests. When I hear the English word supplicate, I think of something like communion, a joining together for the purpose of just being together, to take pleasure in one's relationship with another. Apparently, that is not how Webster's Dictionary defines supplication. Webster defines it as asking or begging for something earnestly or humbly. Our English word, supplication, really fits the idea of the Greek, which is the word *deesos,* which is used for one expressing an urgent personal need. However, do we really need to beg and plead with God for an answer to our prayer? Does it take our earnest pleading and begging to suddenly wake God up to say: "Oh my, poor Chaim really is in a fix? If not for the urgency in His voice, I would have totally disregarded his prayer." God understands our needs better than we do; we don't have to beg and plead to convince Him of the urgency of our need. However, for me personally, the begging and pleading do help get the matter "off my chest," so to speak, and I do feel better once I pour out all my feelings onto God as Hannah did in I Samuel 1. God has already decided how to handle your prayer, but He enjoys listening to your honesty in sharing your heart as much as you just feel comfort in being able to share your heart with Him. There is so much more to a relationship than using that relationship to obtain favors. One great joy in a marriage relationship is knowing you have someone you can go to just to share your heart and know they will listen and offer comfort. It is knowing that there is someone who is truly interested enough in them to listen to the concerns of their hearts. God is such a person you can go to, and He enjoys your heart expression as much as you enjoy expressing your heart to Him. So I am all for Webster's definition of supplication in this verse. Yet, I feel the Aramaic word offers that and more.

The Aramaic word used for supplication, 'on, fits my own personal under-standing of the English word supplication, which is a communion with another. The Aramaic word 'on means to look into, to study, to meditate, or contemplate. In fact, this would be the word to use for contemplative prayer, that is depending on what your definition is of contemplative prayer really is. I would prefer the use of the words silent prayer.

Contemplative prayer has been highly criticized and misunderstood by many orthodox Christians as mystical in nature. They wrongly teach that contemplative prayer is a meditative practice where you focus on a word and repeat the word over and over for the duration of the prayer. This helps clear your mind and opens you up to spiritual revelation. This is not what I or many others are referring to when we speak of contemplative prayer. That is not to say that many who practice contemplative prayer do not in-dulge in such a practice, but it is missing the point of contemplative prayer and throwing the baby out with the bath water, so to speak. In its simplest form, contemplative prayer is prayer in which you still your thoughts and emotions and focus on God Himself, putting yourself in a state where you are aware of God's presence. This would enable you to not only pour your heart out to God but also to hear God's voice of correction, guidance, and direction. Some think the repetition of a word will put them in this state, which is why it has become a practice in contemplative prayer, but I have found that this is not necessary and really distracts from the overall point of contemplative prayer. It is missing the point of contemplative prayer. The fundamental idea is to simply enjoy companionship with God. It is some-times called a prayer of silence.

In my book *Journey Into Silence*, I related my experience of living in silence during a silent retreat at a Benedictine Catholic Monastery in Kentucky.

During this week, when I lived in silence, I was totally off the grid. I spoke to no one, and no one spoke to me. For one week, it was just God and me. During this time, I did not engage in reciting any mantras or repeating a word over and over. I did not spend hours contemplating my navel. Instead, I focused my attention on the God I loved. As Paul exhorts us in Ephesians 6:18, I was *"Praying always with all prayer and supplication in the Spirit."* My life 24/7 was in various states of prayer. I would be in intercessional prayer, personal prayer, the prayer of praise and worship, and silent prayer. It did not take long before I ran out of things to pray or I ran out of words, so I just remained silent before God. I found those times of not speaking to God but just simply enjoying His presence, and I know He was enjoying mine, were really the most precious times on this silent retreat. Just like a loving couple who had been married for many years would just sit on a porch for hours together and say nothing to each other. Yet, they were communicating. They were communicating the joy of being together and enjoying each other's presence. This being silent is just basking in the idea that someone cares enough to just be with you and spend their time with you.

It is during this time that I used the imagination that God created within me. I would imagine Him sitting with me on a log in the forest within the monastery compound, and together we would just be enjoying His creation. I would say nothing to God, and God would say nothing to me, but we would just enjoy being in each other's presence. I would be so relaxed and so at peace, feeling I was wrapped in the arms of a loving God. This is what I am speaking of when I refer to contemplative prayer, just enjoying the presence of God without saying a word. I have attended prayer meetings where someone would open in prayer, and then there would be absolute silence. You could feel the awkwardness. Then the usual people would pray the usual prayer almost identical to the prayer they always prayed in public. I am not saying there is anything wrong with prayers that have been prayed before. There is the awareness of God and the desire to be heard by God and to hear from God. I have no doubt God enjoys hearing the old boy thank Him for his family, job, and all the usual things wrapped up in his prayer. He is, after all, still *palal* - joining himself to God and bringing the rest of the body into this joining with God. What I am saying is sometimes someone will just pray because silence for some reason seems bad, and prayer is not prayer unless someone is speaking. It is almost like that first date where you and your date chatter about anything that comes to mind just to avoid silence like it was some sewer that exists for the sole purpose of being clogged.

The fact is silence before God can be something beautiful. I remember a rabbi teaching that in silence, your heart can hear what your ears cannot hear, your heart can see what your eyes cannot see, and your heart can speak what your mouth cannot speak. I have found that in silence, you can hear the cry of the world. In silence, you can hear, see and feel God weeping for a lost world.

Perhaps this is why Paul separates supplication or *'on* from the major heading of prayer. I believe the Aramaic word *'on* represents silent prayer, a prayer that allows you to hear God's heart as you pour your heart out to Him. Of all forms of prayer, this is the greatest prayer, not saying anything at all but listening to God's heart. As a baby draws comfort from listening to its mother's heartbeat, so too we can draw peace and comfort by listening to our Savior's heart.

14. FERVENT PRAYER

Matthew 6:7: "But when ye pray, use not vain repetitions, as the heathen do: for they think that they shall be heard for their much speaking."

James 5:16: "Confess your faults one to another, and pray one for another, that ye may be healed. The effectual fervent prayer of a righteous man availeth much."

The word in Aramaic here for prayer is *tsala'*, which is the same root for roasting meat or baking. Roasting meat suggests an intensity. *Tsala'* is a great expression of emotions such as sorrow, anger, or urgency, which is often colloquially expressed as heat. Even in English, we speak of a "heated" argument. That is an argument that is filled with passion and anger. When an animal, like a dog, is seeking intimacy with another animal, we say it is in heat. Passion is an expression of heat. Hence the prayer that Jesus is referring to here is one filled with emotion and passion.

Hannah's prayer in I Samuel 1:10: *"And she was in bitterness of soul, and prayed unto the LORD, and wept sore,"* serves as a model for Jewish prayer. She was so passionate in her prayer for a child that the High Priest Eli accused her of being drunk. Here in Hebrew, the word for prayer is again *palal*, that notch in a tent peg. In Hannah's prayer, she was tightly clinging to the notch in that peg or anchor.

James talks about the effectual fervent prayer. The King James translators chose the English word fervent because it expressed a display of passionate intensity. Most Greek scholars teach that the word for effectual fervent, which is *energoumene,* would be better rendered as energetic, passionate,

81

sincere, hearty, and/or earnest. It involves words that flow from one's very heart and soul. Some commentators suggest that it is a reference to the kind of prayer that is motivated by the Spirit of God.

In the Aramaic, the word used for effectual fervent is *chayl*, which is an intense concentration of power and resources. Again, this is the idea of a passionate expression of one's heart and soul. *Chayl* is a form of dancing that was considered an expression of worship and praise. It has the idea of spinning in a circle as a child will spin around in a circle out of pure joy. In fact, *chayl* was a form of worship for children by spinning themselves in a circle. I recall attending a worship service, and in the midst of the worship, which allowed for a free expression of one's joy and love for God, I saw a small child, no more than five or six years old, run into the aisle of the sanctuary and just spin around in a circle out of pure joy. She was just expressing the deep passion she felt, and spinning in a circle was the release of that passion.

To really express your true passion, you need to focus intensely on the object of your passion. I recall hearing an art historian speak of an elderly curator at an Art Museum in France who told him that as a child, he met the great impressionist painter Monet. He told how, one cold winter day, he and his father took a walk along the frozen Rhine River. His father said: "I bet we will meet Monet today." Sure, enough, they came upon Monet, an elderly man sitting on a stool before an art easel, painting some scene that captured his attention. As they approached, Monet stood up to greet them, and as he did, he took off his hat. It was well below zero outside on that lake, and this curator, even as a small child, was amazed to see steam rising from Monet's head when he removed his hat. Monet had been so passionate, so *chayl* – intense in his painting that he actually worked up a sweat in that subzero temperature. That is the idea behind a fervent, passionate prayer.

Some years ago, I worked for a healing evangelist, and I recall standing in the healing line as people came forward to be prayed over for some physical healing. A young man came up to me and said he had cancer and asked that I pray for his healing.

I suddenly felt very insecure about praying for this individual because I felt no real passion or fervency to pray for his condition. I prayed to God and said, "God, I don't know this guy; I never met him before. I have no idea what he is going through. How can I really pray a passionate, fervent prayer for him? Instantly, I was struck with a sharp, debilitating pain in my back.

It literally took the breath out of me. I asked the young man where his pain was, and he pointed to his back at the same spot where I felt the pain in my back. I realized at that moment that sometimes you must be willing to walk the path of the one you are praying over to actually offer a fervent, passionate prayer.

We tend to go to one of two extremes when it comes to prayer. There are those who say you should only pray for something once and then just leave it alone; no need to keep praying for something once you have made it known to God. Then there is the other extreme, which instructs us to pray continually for something over and over, don't give up praying; your persistence will finally win through. Jesus is not referring to those who are constantly praying for something, nor is He saying that you need only to ask once. He is making a reference to the sincerity of our prayers.

Some people just pray out of obligation. I ran into this all the time when I was a pastor. For some reason, my seminary degree and ordination as a minister of the Gospel made me the "go-to guy" to give an invocation, to offer a blessing for a meal, or to start off some business meeting with a word of prayer. How often have I heard the words, "Let's invite the Lord into this meeting," as if he were not already present? I would then need to offer some words which sounded pious and holy to relieve everyone's conscience that we did our duty and gave our proper loyalty oath, like a pledge of alliance to some flag. Did anyone actually listen to my holy words? Did God? If you were God, would you listen to these words?

Normally, they were the same old same old. "Father, we thank you for the blessings of this day...." I recall one deacon who was so caught off guard to open a meeting in prayer that he really did not have a chance to formulate the right words, and he began his prayer for this business meeting with, "Lord, we thank you for this food."

We treat God like some insecure dictator who needs constant reassurance that He is wonderful and deserving of our loyalty. So, like faithful subjects, our words are filled with all sorts of praise and fine words meant to impress not only our "celestial dictator" but those around us who are listening in.

I get a lot of praise for my books and some of the things I write. Sometimes it is sincere, but many times I sense the praise is more patronizing. The words are kind and helpful but often seem very condescending to the point of just simple flattery. That is, the words seem almost like excessive compliments for the purpose of ingratiating oneself to me.

God is not so insecure that He needs to surround Himself with a lot of yes people who will praise and honor just to ingratiate themselves to Him. Our praise and worship are only acceptable to God when it is given with a heart filled with love and adoration. When we love someone, we just need to express that love. Worship and praise are more for us and our need to express our love for God than it is for God's ego.

Along the same lines, we do not flatter God with a lot of vain words and much speech on how wonderful He is just to get an answer to our prayer. In fact, such words are an abomination to Him. He is more interested in the sincerity of our hearts and the words that flow from our hearts.

May we never pray one word that our hearts have not first spoken.

Fervency in prayer does not have to come from personally experiencing one's difficulty; it can also come from just a sense of compassion and empathy for someone just by observing one's situation. God can use many ways to help us observe someone's circumstances, like dreams and visions.

I had a woman who rode on my disability bus; we will call her Patricia. She is the same age as I am, just a couple of months older. So, I am aware that I must respect my elders. But I will be nice. Seriously, she really is a good person. She may be kind of rough around the edges, tattoo, barfly type who has a good heart. She is the one who takes in stray, homeless cats and things like that. She is single, and her children live in another state, but she fiercely maintains her independence despite having crippling arthritis.

I enjoy driving her as she is a very gentle, sensitive lady, almost childlike. She is the type you just want to hug and protect if she were not so fiercely independent. I tried to talk to her about God and her relationship with Him, but she was on to other things and quite uninterested. Anyways I assured her of my prayers, and I told her that if she ever really found herself in need, just reach her arms out to God and say, "Please come help me."

I last drove Patricia in the early Fall of last year. I had not seen her until recently. Around January, I picked up a woman from her apartment complex, and I asked about Patricia as I had not driven her for some time. She told me that she was in the hospital, had been in the hospital for some weeks, and they were planning to put her into a nursing home if she lived. I felt so bad for her, probably because she was my age, and but for the grace of God, go I. I admit I did not think of her much after that, nor did I pray for her.

Yet, a couple of weeks later, I had this dream. I was in the hospital room with Patricia and her doctor. Her doctor told her she would likely never walk again. She had no feeling in her legs. I remember in the dream kneeling by her bedside and crying out to God: "Oh Lord, she doesn't deserve this, show her how real you are to her, let her walk onto my bus again someday. Oh, God, come help my friend, come help my friend." I remember I felt like I was like a little child running to his father and saying: "Daddy, my friend needs some help. Come help my friend." I recall the fervency in my prayer in that dream, and I awoke in tears. I remember thinking: "Wow! Where did that dream come from?"

After a few months, I was checking over my list of passengers that I would be picking up on my disability bus, and I saw the name Patricia Alexander. I was honestly excited over the prospect of seeing her and finding out how she was doing. I drove up to her apartment complex, and there she was on the steps waiting for me. When I got there, I jumped out of the bus as I figured she would need some help. But when she walked toward me, I almost ran over and hugged her. Of course, I would not do that. For one thing, I am on the autistic spectrum, and I don't do hugs. Also, that would be grounds for sexual harassment nowadays. But I just stood there and said, "It is so wonderful to see you walking without a walker." She asked how I knew about her condition, and I quickly explained her neighbor told me about what was going on, although I knew nothing about her how serious her condition was. I didn't mention my dream as I didn't want her to think I was crazy. But then I blurted out, "I've been praying for you."

She smiled and said: "Well, then I guess I can tell you as you won't think I'm crazy. Everyone I tell this to thinks I'm crazy, but I'm not." She then explained that her condition had worsened so badly that she could not even pick up a fork to feed herself. A nurse had to feed her. Then one day, the doctor came into the room and told her that she would probably never be able to move her legs and walk again. After the doctor left, she said she did what I told her to do, and she reached and cried out to God to let her walk again. Then all of a sudden, she moved her left leg, then her right leg and the feeling was coming back. Then she got out of bed and walked.

I mean, she is not exactly doing a marathon and does need to walk with a cane, but they gave her a walker, which she said is brand new and still sitting in her apartment. She has never had the need to use it.

I had no idea what the doctor told her and even what she was in the hospital for other than what her neighbor told me and what was revealed to me in my dream. I told her of my dream and my prayer. When we got off the bus, she gave me a hug. Even though I am told I have Asperger's Syndrome, I found no problem receiving her hug because we were just rejoicing in the Name of God and the power of prayer.

I call it a dream prayer. Call it what you want, but God did say that the fervent prayer of a righteous person avails much. I am only righteous through the blood of Jesus, and even the fervency of my prayers comes from just feeling the fervency of the heart of Jesus. God has many ways to create that fervency in your prayers.

15. DOES GOD REWARD US WITH ANSWERED PRAYER?

Genesis 15:1: "After these things the word of the LORD came unto Abram in a vision, saying, Fear not, Abram: I am thy shield, and thy exceeding great reward."

Ruth 2:12: "The LORD recompense thy work, and a full reward be given thee of the LORD God of Israel, under whose wings thou art come to trust."

Psalms 91:8: "Only with thine eyes shalt thou behold and see the reward of the wicked."

If you read the story of Abram (later named Abraham), you will discover that the words "after these things" are a reference to the account of Abraham rescuing his nephew Lot from the four kings and claiming a great victory in a war against them. So here he is, a victorious warrior and leader, and the word of the Lord came to him in a vision saying, "Fear not." I would expect this vision to come before Abram took his band of untrained servants to go against seasoned warriors who totally outnumbered him. Yet, here he is, coming off the throes of a great victory. I mean, this old boy had to really be pumped. Then the Lord says, "Fear not." If there is one time to not be fearful, it would be this time. Abram had all the proof he needed to know that God was capable and able to protect him and his family and give him great victories to boot.

What was Abram fearful about? Well, the rest of the verse seems to imply that he would not get a reward. This is even more disturbing. If you read the story of Abram, you will find that money and reward were not his goal in life. He did come into great riches which were given to him by God, but that is not what he was all about. Or did I read his biography wrong? Was this guy really a mercenary serving God because God paid him so well?

I recall the first time I ever heard what we call a prosperity teacher. This is a preacher who teaches that God wants you to be prosperous, and all you have to do to tap into his cattle on a thousand hills is to give him what little money you have, and the Lord will bless you a hundredfold. This preacher was brought in by the church's denominational leadership to help raise funds for a new addition to be added to the church building.

This old boy would travel around the world speaking to churches. He had a really great track record of raising funds for churches while keeping back a significant fund for expenses, you know. You can't be a prosperity teacher if you are not prosperous yourself. We were told how lucky we were to get this guy as he was really in demand and how we should really show our appreciation in the *sacar* (payment, reward) way.

Oh, yeah, I forgot to mention the word for reward that is used in our study verse is *sacar,* which means wages, financial and material gain. That's right, Abram had to be history's greatest prosperity teacher. Anyway, this teacher visiting our church quoted Malachi 3:7:10, the hallmark verse on prosperity teaching:

> *Bring ye all the tithes into the storehouse, that there may be meat in mine house, and prove me now herewith, saith the LORD of hosts, if I will not open you the windows of heaven, and pour you out a blessing, that there shall not be room enough to receive it.*

Then he proceeded to retell the old Bible stories we learned in Sunday school with a little different twist. He emphasized that young David had heard about the reward for killing Goliath, and the more he heard, the more he got really pumped. He even asked around to make sure what the reward was proving, according to this preacher, that there is nothing wrong in serving God for a reward. The preacher gave a good, compelling argument for the fact that the road to prosperity is found in your tithes and offerings.

The idea that you will prosper if you pay your tithe and you will not prosper if you don't has worked very well in building churches and ministries and has actually become part of the dogma of church teachings, at least in the sense of paying your tithe. You pay your part to God; He will pay you; you scratch his back, He will scratch yours; you put a dime in God's slot machine, and you will get three bars every time. Santa Claus does exist, we call Him God, and He is making a list and checking it twice to find out who is naughty or nice to determine who gets the blessings and who doesn't.

It all makes sense (culturally speaking), and it seems the Bible supports it, at least from the standpoint of our modern translations. Yet, deep in my spirit, I just feel there is something very wrong about this. I related a story in an earlier chapter where I sat under the teaching of a prosperity teacher and refused to make a pledge, only to discover had I made a pledge, I would have one of the best testimonies in that church on how God prospered me. This confirmed my deep inner conviction that this idea of giving to get is a bit wacky.

I just sensed that the Lord was telling me, "I don't make deals. I don't accept bribes. You can't buy Me, and you can't manipulate Me. I will bless you when I want to bless you. I am not an ATM, I am not a slot machine in a casino, nor am I a computer program. I am your creator, and I have created you to have everything you need to accomplish your mission on earth." In other words, we cannot bribe God into answering our prayers by giving our tithes and offerings.

I have heard some preachers even refer to it as "paying" our tithes and offerings. When I hear the word paying, I think of receiving merchandise in return for the payment of a price. Paying our tithes and offerings to me suggests that we are paying God to answer our prayers. As much as I support our capitalistic system in this country, I do not find that God is a capitalist.

I remember years ago, I got on a bus in Chicago, and as I was traveling to my destination, some old boy stood up with a handful of different colored handkerchiefs. He announced that his bishop had blessed these pieces of cloth and that he was selling them for various prices. The blue ones were for a financial blessing, the red ones for a healing, the green ones for restored relationships, and so forth. Each one had a different price. The most expensive one was for healing. The blue ones for a financial blessing had a variable price depending upon the amount of financial blessing you were seeking. All you had to do was purchase one of these handkerchiefs and pray for the blessing that you wanted, and your prayer would be answered. Sounds crazy, no? Yet, people in desperation fall for it without even realizing that God's love cannot be purchased.

Yet, what about this Malachi 3:10 business? Does not the Lord say to "test Him" and see if He does not open the windows of heaven and pour out blessings? Well, let's examine this idea of a tithe. The word tithe in Hebrew is *ma'eser* from the root word *'eser*, which means a tenth or a complete unit. The purpose of the tithe, as related in the key verses of Deuteronomy 14:22-26 and Leviticus 27:30, speaks of bringing food to the temple for the members of the tribe of Levi, who were the priestly tribe and were not granted any land to grow their food. Their portion was God; that is that they were to spend their time studying Torah, teaching, ministering, and serving in the temple. They had no time or land to grow their food. There were no grocery stores, nor did they have any money to go to market and purchase food. They were wholly dependent upon the tithes of the other eleven tribes, who brought a tenth of their crops to the temple for the sole purpose of feeding the people of the tribe of Levi.

The practice of giving a tithe was really considered a tax. This is where Jesus almost ran into trouble when a pharisee asked if he should pay taxes to the Roman government. The words tax and tithe were used interchangeably because it was a practice by governments to charge a 10% tax. To the Jews, paying a 10% tax to the government was the same as paying a tithe, and you only tithed to the Lord, not the government.

After the destruction of the Temple, the tithe was no longer needed as the tribe of Levi no longer served a function, and hence, they started to earn their own living. I even heard one rabbi say that if his congregation were to start tithing, it would be a sin. He indicated that a tithe was only meant for the Temple and nothing else. Jews do not tithe; they support their synagogue and rabbi through paying dues, like membership dues and offerings.

The point of this is that giving to the Lord or the Lord's work is not an obligation, not a duty, not a law; it is just an act of one's free will. We can call it a freewill offering or a love gift. It is meant to show our love to God, the act of giving and not expecting anything in return.

This brings me back to this fellow known as Abram, who loved God with all his heart, soul, and might. He served God out of love, not expecting anything in return other than knowing that his God was pleased with Him. He loved God beyond his own life and the life of his beloved son. Maimonides, the great Medieval Jewish commentator, singles out Abraham as the poster child of serving God out of pure love. The idea that Abram, a man so devoted to God, would be concerned about a piece of the action just stretches the imagination. The Talmud in Avot 1:3 teaches that we are to be like a servant who serves his master without being motivated by attaining a reward. In other words, we should seek to live a righteous life, not to obtain heaven, not obtain special favors from God but to just express our love to Him.

In Christianity, the reward seems to be the goal. We are all seeking heaven; we want to go up when the rapture occurs. Let me ask you something and answer within your own heart. If, just before the rapture, Jesus appears and says He is going to give you a choice. You can be raptured out of this world, enter heaven, join in the marriage supper of the Lamb, and have joy and peace and all that other good stuff, or you can choose to stay behind for the seven-year tribulation period where you will have to endure great hardship, persecution and possibly torture for your faith. However, you will have the power of God and the presence of the Holy Spirit like never before to lead others to the Lord. Which would you choose?

I often asked this question to my students when I was teaching in Bible college. Some actually said they would take the rapture, acting like I was some sort of fool to believe anyone would choose otherwise. Some, realizing the "trick" question, would hem and haw and say that God would never give us that choice. He would never subject the ones He loves to such things. I guess we need to just ignore the fact that He subjected His very Son to extreme torture and torment for our sake.

For many such Christians, the answer to our question regarding our study verse is easy. Of course, Abraham was concerned about his reward. Who would not be? God called him to leave his home, his land, and all he knows to move to a foreign and strange land, yet bet your bottom dollar that he expected some sort of reward. Our study verse only shows that God had to remind Abram to hang in there; his reward is coming.

In my search for an answer to the question about Abraham, I searched Jewish literature. Jewish teachers insist that we do not serve God for financial reward. They will not even discuss heaven for fear that they may end up serving God just to secure a seat on the train to heaven, and that becomes their motive for serving God. We Christians talk about heaven as a reward, and although we believe our ticket is already bought and paid for by Jesus, we still seek to serve God to get a bigger mansion. Maybe even a mansion in a star-studded community next door to Peter or Jacob. I have heard it said after the passing of a well-known evangelist or Bible teacher that he was so great that his mansion would be one of the biggest in heaven. Some even go so far as to say he would live in a section of heaven reserved only for the elite. My goodness, that means that even heaven has a gated community to separate God's elite from the riff-raff like Chaim Bentorah. I probably would not even be worthy of being a security guard at one of those gates. That is definitely not a Jewish teaching. If it is not a Jewish teaching, then how do they reconcile this study verse to their description of Abram as a man who served God only out of love?

Well, the first thing is that the Jews have no problem with wealth or prosperity. God chooses who is to be rich and who is to be poor. Nor do they have a problem with pursuing wealth. If you recall the movie or play Fiddler on the Roof, you have the scene where Tevye is singing "If I Were A Rich Man." He first sings of how he would take care of his wife and his family, then his community, but when it comes to himself personally, he sings: "If I were rich, I would have the time to that I lack to sit in the synagogue and pray and maybe have a seat by the Eastern wall. I would discuss the holy books seven hours every day, and that would be the sweetest thing of all." If God made you rich, what would be the sweetest thing of all for you?

Once again, I turn to Maimonides, who suggests that Abram was not interested in the reward itself, but in something that the reward signified. Many times, in an athletic event, the reward for winning a race is not very tangible. Maybe a little trophy or a ribbon. You could purchase something like that on your own. Of course, that would have no meaning because you didn't earn it. The real reward is having achieved the goal that was set before you. That ribbon or trophy is only a tangible sign of what you accomplished.

I saw a picture the other day of President Eisenhower in his military uniform. It showed he was wearing his five stars as a general, but even though he was the most decorated general in United States history, he chose only to wear his top two awards that I believe were awarded to him for D-Day. I read that it was a tradition for soldiers to wear only the wings they were awarded for being in Airborne and not their other ribbons saying: "I'm Airborne, and that is all you need to know."

My point is that the ribbons, medals, and other decorations are only a sign of accomplishment. The true reward is just knowing you passed all the tests and requirements to be Airborne or that you successfully accomplished the most important mission in your life, as with President Eisenhower. Eisenhower was not, of course, the only one responsible for D-Day, but he did give the order to launch. Still, the victory was bittersweet, for he was aware of the many who lost their lives in the invasion that he gave the order to take place. Maybe that has something to do with why he chose not to wear the awards of all his military accomplishments except for those involving D-Day. I don't know the answer to that. But I do see a parallel with Abram, who led a great military victory. Only someone like President Eisenhower could really understand the emotions, the nagging questions that maybe more lives could have been saved had he made different decisions. I believe that day haunted him all his life as in his quiet moments, he pondered alternatives he could have followed in that invasion.

The word for afraid in the Hebrew that is used in Genesis 15:1 is *yara*, which is a fear, not for one's own safety but a fear for the effect you have on others. I believe Abram, although feeling relieved at the outcome of the war against the four kings, felt some sense of *yara*, a sense that maybe if he did something different, maybe if he had a different attitude, so many lives would not have been lost. But God said: "Don't be afraid; I am your shield." The word shield in Hebrew is *magen* from the root word *ganan*, which is an enclosed garden. A fence, so to speak. In other words, God is telling Abram, "I am your fence; I will guard you from any regrets or guilt you may feel or have to bear as a result of this conflict. Once more, your reward will be great."

God was going to give rewards to Abram, not because Abram craved and needed material things, but to remind Abram that he was on the right track. Rewards were only a signpost that he was in the center of God's will, little love gifts from God to remind him that he was safely in God's plan. I watched a dog in an airport video trained to sniff out drugs. As soon as he found the scent of some drugs, he alerted his master in some tangible way. The master then slipped him a little treat, but not without some hugs, and "Who's the good boy?" Did the dog sniff out those drugs for the treats or for the positive approval of his master? I don't know, but I would like to think that positive approval was more a reward than the treat.

Brother Andrew, who, at the risk of his life, smuggled many Bibles into countries that outlawed God and His Word, said: "The safest place to be is in the center of God's will." You know you are in the center of God's will because He will give you little rewards to remind you that you are doing good and to keep you encouraged. Maybe that reward is not really a tangible "treat." It might be just that sweet presence of God and the knowledge that He is delighted with you. In fact, the word for reward, *sacar*, is almost identical to the word *shacar*, which means gifts. God will give you little gifts along your life's journey as signposts that you are headed in the right direction. Do you ever just suddenly feel God's presence for no reason at all? You just are suddenly struck with the overwhelming sweetness of His Spirit. That is one of His gifts. If he handed you a ten-dollar bill, what is your joy? Is it that ten dollars, or is it that He cared enough to give it to you?

Ok, maybe God will give you $100 if you give $10 dollars to some Christian work. But you did not get that $100 from God as a payment for your gift; you got it as a sign from God that you are headed in the right direction.

I have found two words in Hebrew that are rendered as reward. The first is *maskoreth*, found in Ruth 2: 12: *"The LORD recompense thy work, and a full reward be given thee of the LORD God of Israel, under whose wings thou art come to trust."* The second is found in Psalms 91:8 and is the word *shillumath*. Of course, in these Old Testament study verses, *maskoreth* is in reference to a righteous person named Ruth, and *shillumath* is what an evil person will receive. In both cases, the idea of a reward is a payment. The payment of the righteous versus the payment of the wicked. However, in English, the word reward is often a good thing, and when used for something bad, it is used in the sense of lampooning or joking, tongue in cheek, so to speak. Generally, when we think of a reward, we think of something that is given in recognition of one's service or achievement.

What is curious is that the word reward in Psalms 91:8 is *shillumath* from the root word *shelem*, which is the same root where we get the word peace – *shalom*. Peace is a good thing; why would the wicked get peace? In its very Semitic root, the word *shelem* or *shlm*, in its root has the idea of harmonizing. To harmonize is to create a relationship characterized by a lack of conflict or by agreement as of opinion or interest. Hence *shalom* or *shelem* can have a negative idea. That is, wickedness will find a relationship with something that it is in agreement with its wicked acts. In other words, the reward of the wicked is wickedness that the wicked themselves will experience.

What is interesting is that Ruth was blessed with a "full reward." The word reward here is *maskoreth* from the root word *sakar,* which is the word for wages, payment in return for services that are rendered. However, in its Semitic origins, it is used for a dam, causing water to fill a basin. In other words, it has the idea of filling a void, an emptiness, or need. The word full in Hebrew is *shalomah*, the feminine form of the word shalom. Thus, the blessing Ruth was to receive would be to fill a void in her life, but that fulfillment would be harmonious with her need to be filled. She would not only find a husband to care for her, as was the goal of a woman in that culture, but she would have the added bonus of a husband who would love her and cherish her as well. Most men in those days did their duty as a husband, but not all did it out of love and longing to bring happiness and fulfillment to their mate.

We live in a capitalistic culture, which works because it meets that primal need to get some compensation for our efforts. What did Ruth do to deserve her full reward? She was kind to her mother-in-law Naomi. Wow! So just being kind to someone will bring about recompense and reward. That is simple enough, drop a few coins in the fast food paper cup (extra-large) carried by that old down-and-out boy knocking at your car window when you get off the expressway, and you've earned some sort of reward. Is that what *sakar* and *shelem* mean? That seems to be more like karma, cause and effect.

The Jewish Midrash and the Talmud spend a considerable amount of time discussing this issue of rewards *sakar* filling a void and *shelem* filling that void with something harmonious. For one thing, the kindness Ruth shows is part of the law of God to care for your elders. The sages teach that there is no reward for keeping the law of God. That is to say that there is no filling a void in your life with something harmonious with your life if that is your purpose for keeping the law of God. That would be using God's law as bribery. God doesn't have to bribe someone to behave and follow His laws. That should be something we do out of love for God. Ruth was a Moabite who converted to Judaism. She voluntarily submitted herself to the laws of God. She did not have to do this. She just fell in love with God and wanted to obey His laws. But since she did not have to do it and since she did it for no reward, Boaz blessed her by declaring that God would reward her.

The Midrash sets forth a principle that the most desirable component in doing a virtuous deed is the service of the heart. In the Talmud, Sanhedrin 106b, we learn that God desires good deeds to flow from the heart, from love, not the expectation of reward. Sure, we know all this, but do we really?

When it comes to seeking an answer to prayer, how often do we try to bribe or manipulate God with good deeds? For many, the reward, such as answered prayer or even heaven, is their motivation for doing good deeds. They drop a few dollars in that old boy's fast food paper cup (extra-large size) and think: "Well, God will mark that up as a good deed when I make my requests known unto the Lord. Now God will surely answer my prayer." Millions of people attend church every Sabbath because they think that they will somehow bribe God into answering their prayer requests for a new job, financial security, or whatever they are praying for. They think they richly deserve to enter those pearly gates of heaven because they made an effort to attend a religious service and recited some words most likely meaningless to them. But they met the obligation and fully expected their reward. Ephesians 2:8-9 clearly teaches it is by grace we are saved and not of works. Why are we not saved by our good works? Paul gives the answer right in that verse, "Lest any man should boast." Some people love to sound the trumpets when they perform a good deed. They expect a library or a church addition to be named after them if they give a generous enough gift.

That word, *shelem* or *shalom,* is commonly rendered as peace. Peace is a good feeling, a feeling of wholeness and satisfaction. The Lord's reward for doing good deeds is peace. Even the unrighteous feel good after performing some honorable deed. Al Capone started a soup kitchen and gave a lot of money to the poor and needy, and we all know his testimony. But doing those deeds made him feel good. He did it for that warm and fuzzy feel-good feeling and the respect that he felt he was receiving. He saw himself as some sort of Robin Hood or hero, not a criminal or murderer.

We could render Ruth 2:12 as receiving "full wages." Full wages are enough to feed, clothe and find shelter, fulfilling the basic needs to give you a sense of peace. Note the wages that Ruth earned. The Lord God gave her peace under His wings or protection. The word wings is always used as a metaphor for protection. Really, if you have the protection of God, what more do you need? You will live in peace knowing nothing will harm you or come against you that the Lord is not aware of and is not ready to protect you.

But keep in mind, Ruth asked for none of this. She only wanted to take care of her mother-in-law. She only wanted to do what was right for the two people she loved the most, Naomi and God. God's *sakar*— reward or payment was not expected and was just the cherry on top. When you serve God, are you doing it with your heart in your hand or with a greasy palm?

The Jews speak of the commandments of God and law of God, yet when they speak of performing and obeying these commandments and laws, they say that they are performing a mitzvah, which basically means a good deed. Although the literal meaning of mitzvah is commandment, the word really expresses a sense of heartfelt sentiment beyond mere legal duty. It is performing this requirement of the commandment or law out of love for God, not out of obligation or to bribe or manipulate God.

Many Christians not only say but insist that the Jews do not believe in heaven or an afterlife. As evidence, they will say that you will never hear a Jew talk about heaven. "How sad," they would say with a sigh. Well, the Jews definitely believe in an afterlife, a heaven, although they have different words for it, like the Garden of Eden, Paradise, or even the afterlife. They do not speak about heaven because they want to focus on their mission here on Earth. Once you start talking about heaven and trying to get there, suddenly, all your good deeds and good works are being performed to earn you a place in paradise. The Jews take a sort of let heaven take care of itself attitude; let's just focus on fulfilling our mission and purpose in life without the expectation of some reward.

There was a sign outside a church that read: "God gave ten commandments, not ten suggestions." Actually, that is the very reason the Jews call their good deeds mitzvahs because the ten commandments to them are suggestions. You do not keep the commandments to earn a berth on the train ride to heaven; you keep the commandments because they tell us how God created us and how we can find *sakar*, fill that void in our lives that God created in us and how to *shelem* make that filling of the void harmonious with the way God created us to find fulfillment and happiness not only within ourselves but to bring it to others.

True, we will be rewarded for how we live our lives; we will receive either a good or bad reward that is in harmony with the way we live our lives. There is, however, a fine line between serving God to get a reward or serving God to bribe and manipulate Him into giving you a reward. God will not answer your prayer as a reward; He answers your prayer to fulfill a need to carry out the mission you were sent here on earth to fulfill.

16. PURPOSE OF PRAYER

Deuteronomy 10:20: "Thou shalt fear the LORD thy God; him shalt thou serve, and to him shalt thou cleave, and swear by his name."

"Any man who loves God does not demand that God love him." Baruch Spinoza, 17th Century Dutch Jewish philosopher

"Never come a-callin' with a handful of gimmie and a mouthful of much obliged." Old South Proverb

So, if we do not have to pray to give God a good idea of what type of reward we are looking for after we do all our good things, then why bother praying? Let's look at the story of Job. Job had no understanding of the challenge that took place in heaven between God and the enemy. All he knew was that he lost everything, his wealth, his family, and his health. In Job 2:9, we learn: "Then said his wife unto him, Dost thou still retain thine integrity? curse God, and die." Actually, in the Hebrew, the phrase: "curse God and die" is a question. In other words, Job's wife is asking: "Job, look at you, you've lost everything, you are dying, why are you not cursing God?" Note Job's reply: Job 2:10: *But he said unto her, Thou speakest as one of the foolish women speaketh. What? shall we receive good at the hand of God, and shall we not receive evil? In all this did not Job sin with his lips."* Job is the classic example of what the philosopher Spinoza was addressing. From a natural standpoint, it did not appear Job was very loved by God. Yet, Job did not demand God's love, did not demand God to prove His love by restoring him; he just loved God and did not demand anything in return.

That concept does not fit our Western culture of self-gratification. Our whole concept of evangelization is to encourage people to get saved to improve their lives and not go to hell. I once had a rabbi tell me: "Between you and me, I believe life continues after we die. Yeah, there is a heaven, as you call it. But I don't preach it. Once I do, then people will start serving God to get to heaven."

I know a young woman who married a man who turned out to be an alcoholic and drug addict. He would abuse her in many ways, cheat on her, and would spend the family income needed for food and clothes for his two children on himself for drugs and alcohol. Many tried to encourage this young woman to leave her husband and divorce him. There were men who were ready to step in and take care of her and her children. Yet, she would not divorce him, and when asked why, there would be this long pause as she would go into deep thought, and then she would respond, "I love him."

Some people would even declare that there was something psychologically wrong with this woman, that she would continue to love a man who did not return that love. Well, if there is something psychologically wrong with someone who will love when that love is not returned, then there is something psychologically wrong with God. God loves a world that does not love Him in return. In fact, He sent His Son to die for this world that despised Him.

In John 3:16, we learn that God loves the world. In the Aramaic, which is the language that Jesus spoke, the word He used for *love* is *chav*. This is a love that is not necessarily returned. It is a natural love like a mother has for her child, even when that child spits at her and declares he hates her. Yet in John 13:23, we have the words, "The disciple whom Jesus loved." Here the word *love* is *racham* in the Aramaic. This is a shared love, a love that is equally shared by two people.

But *chav* also differs from *racham,* as shown in Luke 7:47: "*Wherefore I say unto thee, Her sins, which are many, are forgiven; for she loved much: but to whom little is forgiven, [the same] loveth little."* From this translation, we get the idea that it is better to sin a lot so we can love God more. But in the Aramaic, we find again that the word used for *love* is *chav.* Here we find that *chav* is a lesser love than *racham. Chav* is not only a love that may not be returned; it is also a conditional love. "I love you because…." Jesus made it clear that His real desire was *racham love* which transcends *chav. Racham* is a love that does not expect to be loved in return, but when it is, it becomes the most satisfying form of love because you know you are loved no matter how you may fail. It is a love that is perfect and, well, the Bible explains it best: 1 John 4:18: *"There is no fear in love; but perfect love casteth out fear: because fear hath torment. He that feareth is not made perfect in love."* You never need to fear that if you make a mistake or say the wrong thing, you will lose that love. *Chav,* the love Jesus talked about in Luke 7:47, is a love dependent upon receiving something in return. But his disciples were growing into *racham* love which made them ready to be truly intimate with God. True intimacy is when a couple loves each other so much they do not care if they find personal pleasure in the relationship, yet they find great pleasure in the knowledge that they brought pleasure to the one they love.

If the enemy had a list of ten things that terrifies him the most, right up there on top of the list would be a husband who truly loves his wife, that is a picture of *racham* love. What is worse yet for the enemy is a wife who will return that love. Such a relationship drives the enemy insane because such a relationship exposes the true nature of God's love for us as *racham,* I love you because I want to love you, and not *chav,* I love you because…. The enemy cannot have that, so the first thing he attacks in a culture to drive it away from God is the home. He will flood the market with pornography and lurid jokes about the most beautiful thing God created, to turn it into a selfish, self-gratified, and self-centered form of pleasure.

We now have no-fault divorce in every state. If a man cannot satisfy his wife or the wife satisfy her husband, they are free to divorce to find someone who can. It is almost acceptable and expected that if your mate cannot satisfy you sexually, you are free to find someone who can, and if their mate is hurt and shattered by this, well, just too bad for them; we all have a right to happiness.

Is it any wonder that our modern churches are gradually becoming entertainment halls rather than places of worship? Churches are becoming places to cater to lovers of self rather than places where one can fall on an altar, weep and repent of their sins before God. Can you imagine a church growth program that teaches if you become a Christian, you may lose your job, your home, or even your life? Can you imagine a church growth program succeeding when it teaches that you may end up in prison and tortured? Yet such a church program worked in the first century; it worked in Communist China and the old Soviet Union in the mid-20th Century. It is working in many Middle Eastern countries today because they teach *racham love*, a love that says I love only because I want to love you and not the *chav love* that is so prevalent in America, which says: "I love you because you do so much for me."

I had a student once who came to our Bible college from Russia during the Perestroika reforms. His father had been in prison during the old Soviet persecution of believers, and he himself had suffered persecution under the old system. I asked him why he became a Christian when it was so dangerous. He simply replied: "I love Jesus."

I hear Christians all the time crying out for intimacy with God. But they want that intimacy to feel good, not because they love God with unconditional love. The evidence of that is the way our modern Western English translators translate many verses in the Bible, such as Deuteronomy 10:20: "*Thou shalt fear the LORD thy God; him shalt thou serve, and to him shalt thou cleave, and swear by his name.*" That word *cleave* in Hebrew is *devekut* and is rendered in our modern translations as *cleave, cling, hold fast to, remain faithful, be loyal, hold or adhere to.* Really? I mean, really? Such renderings of the Hebrew word *devekut* are enough to cause any rabbi to throw salt in the air.

Devekut is a very powerful word among Orthodox Jews. It is an extreme joining of oneself with God through a longing and desire to be as close to God as is humanly possible. In fact, there are records of rabbis who so longed and desired to be close to God that they would spend hours communing with God in prayer - *palal* and would actually die while they were communing with God. It was said that they received the *kiss of God*. Do you love Him so much that you long to be *kissed by Him*? Paul said in Philippians 1:21: "*For to me to live [is] Christ, and to die [is] gain.*" In Greek, that word *gain* is like the gain on an annuity. It is the interest that accumulates from the capital. Our life here on earth is just to accumulate the interest that we will live off of in heaven.

So, what is the best English word for *devekut*? To really get down to the very Semitic idea of the word *devekut*, it would be *to give and/or receive a hug or embrace.* I have a friend who is a nurse, and she told me that if you had two babies and you hugged and embraced one baby, that baby would thrive. But if you simply met the needs of the other baby, fed it, changed its diaper, etc., it would die if you never hugged it or embraced it. They are now doing research on the elderly and finding the same effect. In fact, it is proven that if a husband and wife never touched each other, never embraced or hugged each other, that relationship would die. We have a basic human need to be touched and hugged, which is reflective of our need to be touched and hugged by God.

God created the intimacy between a man and woman to be an emotional picture of the intimate relationship he desires with us. Intimacy is at its best when both people seek only to bring happiness and pleasure to the other. They have to give themselves over to each other completely; all their dreams and hopes have to be shared. No secrets, no lies, no hidden agendas, only putting the other person first and sharing every aspect of their hearts with each other.

Eric Liddle, the subject of the movie Chariots of Fire, was a man who was called by God to be a missionary. But he was also gifted by God to run fast. As he was training for the Olympics, he explained to his sister why he was running. He told her: "God made me for a purpose, but He also made me fast. When I run, I feel His pleasure."

God has created us each for a purpose. He also gave each one of us gifts. When we use those gifts, it brings Him pleasure, and we feel His pleasure. Some are gifted musicians; some are gifted mechanics. Some are gifted in gardening and farming. Some are gifted in teaching or preaching. The problem in our culture is that certain gifts receive more honor than others. Hence someone who is a gifted handyman and can fix anything in a church envies that musician who performs with the worship team each Sunday. I had a friend who was a Catholic priest once tell me that when he is in the basement doing woodwork, he feels the presence of God more than when he is offering mass. He was a gifted craftsman, and maybe God created him to be a craftsman rather than a clergyman.

It is important before a couple gets married to really understand what they love about each other. Maybe the woman really wants a man who just wants to own his own home and fix things up around the house. The guy may be a great musician but cares nothing about owning a home and can't even change a light bulb. They will quickly discover that he will not bring her the pleasure she desires and that perhaps they are not meant to be married.

Understanding one's future mate and what their abilities are to make each other happy is fundamental in the development of a relationship and the determination as to whether that relationship will end in marriage or not. Yet, we completely overlook that in our churches. Coveted positions in the church, like serving on the worship team, preaching, and teaching, are portioned out to those based on their loyalties to the church and not their gifts or abilities. We spend so much time concentrating on how we can serve God rather than concentrating on what brings pleasure to God. We say we want to feel the presence of God. Actually, it is feeling the pleasure of God that we really desire, and that comes from being what God created us to be and do.

I recall when I was a Christian Education director, I had to start a boys club that involved camping trips. I hated camping; I was absolutely no good at it. There was a new Christian in our church who was in the special forces in the army. I approached him about leading this boys' program. He was shocked, swore he was not qualified, and did not want to take this wonderful opportunity away from others, particularly myself. To him, to take young men out on a camping trip and guide them was a dream he never felt would come true, but God created him that way. For me, it would have been absolute misery and total failure because God did not create me that way. When he took those boys out camping, he felt God's pleasure and grew into deep intimacy with him such that he shared the Gospel with those boys in a way I could never have.

Therein lies our real purpose in prayer. Remember, the word prayer in Hebrew is *palal,* which is the notch in a tent peg. Prayer is what attaches us or joins us to God. It is love that will draw us to God, and it is prayer that will join us to the one that we love. Ultimately, our purpose in prayer is to join us with the one we love.

17. SAYING TABLE GRACE

Matthew 26:26: "*And as they were eating, Jesus took bread, blessed and broke it, and gave it to the disciples and said, "Take, eat; this is My body."*

Mark 14:22: "*And as they did eat, Jesus took bread, and blessed, and brake it, and gave to them, and said, Take, eat: this is my body."*

Luke 22:17: "*And he took the cup, and gave thanks, and said, Take this, and divide it among yourselves:"*

Matthew 15:36: "*And he took the seven loaves and the fishes, and gave thanks, and brake them, and gave to his disciples, and the disciples to the multitude."*

Matthew 14:19: "*And he commanded the multitude to sit down on the grass, and took the five loaves, and the two fishes, and looking up to heaven, he blessed, and brake, and gave the loaves to his disciples, and the disciples to the multitude."*

II Corinthians 11:24: "*And when he had given thanks, he brake it, and said, Take, eat: this is my body, which is broken for you: this do in remembrance of me."*

Leviticus 14:36: "*Then the priest shall command that they empty the house, before the priest go into it to see the plague, that all that is in the house be not made unclean: and afterward the priest shall go in to see the house."*

A very common blessing and practice is "saying grace" before a meal. Generally, it is a prayer that pretty much follows a script. Maybe not so much the "God is good, God is great, we thank Him for the food we take." But it runs quite similarly. I had a roommate in Bible College who would always open his table grace with: "Lord, we thank you for the blessings of this day." One weekend I visited his home with his family, and his father said grace before the meal, which began with: "Lord, we thank you for the blessings of this day." I know it is hard to be original when you are called upon to recite a simple prayer day after day. I mean, there are only so many ways to express your thankfulness without repeating the same words over and over. Only in heaven will we fully understand just how God feels about these little spot loyalty oaths, but you have to admit, it is His own fault if He is driven to distraction over hearing the same words over and over from the lips of millions of people. I mean, He is the one who instituted table grace.

Above are just a few of the verses that encourage us to say "table grace." Many translations do not see a difference between blessing the bread and giving thanks for the bread. Yet, these Jews who sat with Jesus saw a great difference and one which we, as Christians, really need to consider.

In Matthew 26:26 and Mark 14:22, the word in Greek that is used for bless is *eulogesteo,* where we get our English word for eulogy, which means to speak with praise, to honor. In Aramaic, the word used in these two passages for bless is *barak,* which means to bless, but in its Semitic origins, it has the idea of carving out, standing out, selecting. In Luke 22:17, which speaks of the same occasion, Luke uses a different word in Greek, he uses the word *eucharistie,* where we get the word eucharist that is used for communion, and it means to show grace or favor. In Aramaic, Luke uses the word *'avo di* which has the idea of turning away from evil from anything unclean. It even means to make something from unclean to clean. These words for bless or thanksgiving are the basis for our modern table grace. In Matthew 14:19 and Matthew 15:36, we have another example of Jesus saying table grace before he fed the multitudes. In Matthew 14:19, the word in Greek for bless is *eulogesteo,* and in Matthew 15:36, the word is *eucharistie.* In Aramaic, the word used in Matthew 14:19 is *barach,* but in Matthew 15:36, where Jesus performs the same act only among a different crowd, Matthew uses the word *shavach.* When the Apostle Paul tells this story of the Last Supper in I Corinthians 11:24, he uses the word *eucharistie* for bless, and the Aramaic uses the word *barak.*

Now for some Western purist thinkers, this presents a problem. Simply put, we have an account of the same event, the Last Supper, where Jesus takes bread and breaks it and says a blessing or gives thanks. Yet Matthew and Mark use the word *eulogesteo* for blessing or thanksgiving, and Luke uses a different word in Greek eucharistie. "Aha," says the skeptic, "Lookie here, the same account yet two different words; Jesus could not have used both words for the one event; therefore, either Matthew and Mark made an error in their record, or Luke made an error. See there, you fanatical, illogical fundamentalists who believe the Bible is inerrant; we have a glaring error right before your eyes."

The response to that is quite easy, "Stop thinking like a Platonic, Western, technological, mathematical, scientific scholar who is sitting up in his ivy tower of academia. Ask him about the color of his wife's eyes. He will not say, 'It is a soft glowing turquoise like the sky on a crisp autumn day.' He will likely say, 'It's blue or green or something like that.' If he even knows the color of his wife's eyes." You see, Luke was listening to Jesus's words with his heart, as were Matthew and Mark. When they recorded the event, they recorded their heart's record, and the difference in words only gives us a greater depth of understanding of the heart of Jesus 2,000 years later. We can argue the difference in nuances because the Koine Greek which is a dead language and discuss how much was lost in its death, not to mention the shaving off of meanings when we put it into a modern language like English. Not only that, Jesus spoke an Old Galilean form of Aramaic, not Greek, so this has gone through two translations from Aramaic to Greek to English. You lose a lot in translations. Not only that, the only Aramaic record we have is the Peshitta, which was written in Syriac, an Aramaic dialect. We have no records of the Old Galilean that Jesus spoke. So, it is very easy to argue that no error was committed in the use of different words; God only allowed the story to be repeated to help us understand what was going through the minds of the writers and what Jesus was trying to express. *Eucharistie* and *eulogesteo* both have the common idea and/or meaning of to strengthen, enhance or show favor.

In Aramaic, we have three different words used for saying a prayer before a meal. We have *barak*, which is to give a blessing but also means to strengthen, make strong. You have *shavach*, which means to enhance the value of something, and you have *'avodi,* which means to turn from evil and make something pure. All these words carry a common denominator or meaning of making something special. When you give thanks for a meal, you are making it special by recognizing this meal is brought to you by the courtesy of God. Holy means to be separate and/or special.

You can eat a fried chicken dinner cooked by grandma, and maybe it doesn't have all the spices of Kentucky Fried Chicken and might not have that snappy taste of KFC, but it tastes good because grandma made it with love. The fact that she purchased the raw chicken, defrosted it, added the breading, fried it herself, and took the time to lovingly fry it to perfection makes that dinner special or holy, far more special or holy than some teenager who tosses a bunch of chicken into a deep fat fryer and sets the alarm to tell him when to take it out. There is no love there. It was only made by some teenager hidden away kitchen from you, who never sees you nor even cares about you; he just wants his paycheck so he can purchase a car to take his date to the movies. But if you purchased that fried chicken from KFC, you can still make it special or holy by saying a *eucharistie, eulogesteo, shavach, 'avodi, barak* (choose the word you want) over it because you recognize that it came from God. He created that chicken who gave its life for you, he gave you the finances to purchase that KFC meal, and he gave you a healthy stomach to keep you from getting a stomach ache from eating all that grease.

Let's find one word that fits the context of table grace for *eucharistie, eulogesteo, shavach, 'avodi, barak.* I personally would choose the word *kodesh,* which feel fits quite nicely. What are you doing when you give thanks for your meal? You are making it *kodesh* or holy. That is, you are making it different than any other meal that people eat all over the world. You are making that meal holy with that table blessing, that table grace. You are separating it from everything else and holding it out as a special gift from God.

My grandmother used to make sourdough biscuits every other Sunday. You see, my two grandmothers, my father's mother, and my mother's mother lived a block away from each other which was a block away from the church we attended every Sunday. My father married the girl next door whom he met at church. So, every Sunday, we went to dinner at grandma's house. One week it would be my mother's mother, and the next week it would be my father's mother. So, every other Sunday, we would delight in grandma's southern-style cooking for my father's mother, who grew up down South. She made the best biscuits I had ever eaten, and believe me, I have eaten every possible biscuit I could get my hands on, trying to find one that tasted as good as grandma's. I have been to many different restaurants, southern-style restaurants, and restaurants that even posted signs saying they had the best southern-style biscuits in the world. None came close to grandma's biscuits.

You see, my grandma would get up at 3:00 am to begin making those biscuits. She would start by shifting her own flour, using her own starter passed down by her mother, who received it from her mother, sort of like apostolic succession. She did not attend church that Sunday; her sabbath was celebrated by preparing a meal for the ones she loved. I daresay she prayed over every ingredient (making it holy). I have no doubt she and God had a more special time together than many of us would have had at a church service (no offense to a church service, you understand). She kept her Sabbath holy by just loving her family.

By the time our pastor finished that long commercial at the end of the church service, my imagination was so keen that I could smell those biscuits in the oven. I had a great imagination back then. The pastor's Amen was just a prelude to another prayer that my family and I would have within the next hour. That prayer was called table grace, where grandma reminded us that this meal was holy as unto the Lord. Anyone outside our family eating those biscuits would say, "They are good, almost like KFC, which has the best biscuits." Grandma's biscuits had an ingredient that KFC did not have, two measures of love, grandma's and God's, and that was her secret recipe that made those biscuits the best I have ever eaten anywhere in my 70 years of walking this earth.

So often before a meal when we hear the host ask someone to say "the blessing" or to give thanks for the meal. This is indeed what Jesus was doing, no matter what words are used to express this in the Greek or Aramaic. Jesus was making that bread holy, which made it just as special as grandma's biscuits. Even if it is the same old "Thank you for the blessings of this day…" prayer, at least you are acknowledging God's role and presence no matter what words you use.

But, you may have noticed I have a passage from Leviticus among our study verses. Leviticus 14:36:

> *Then the priest shall command that they empty the house, before the priest go into it to see the plague, that all that is in the house be not made unclean: and afterward the priest shall go in to see the house.*

So, what does this passage speaking of calling a priest to examine one's house for the sign of a plague have to do with table grace? It has a lot to do with table grace.

You see, this command to the Hebrews to examine their house for the sign of the plague *tzara'at,* which the Jewish rabbis say is incorrectly translated as leprosy, was to take effect when they entered the Promised Land, the land of Canaan. What happened was that they moved into the land and forced the inhabitants of the land to flee from their homes, taking only what they could carry and leaving behind the rest. Rather than build new homes, the Hebrews just occupied the existing homes. However, these homes were dedicated to pagan gods; I believe demonic beings who passed themselves off as gods. Some or many of these houses were owned by faithful servants or even dedicated servants of the pagan gods that actually performed and spoke words of praise and worship to these demonic beings in these homes. These words were embedded in these homes, so to speak. They were dedicated to demonic beings, and there had to be a purification of these homes. Some ignored these purification ceremonies and took up residence. Well, God put a mark on these homes, and it was the duty of the new owners to report these marks to a priest. If they didn't, the marks would appear on their clothing, and if they still ignored this warning, the marks or skin disease would appear on their bodies. These marks were called the signs of *tzara'at* or leprosy. The priest would come, and if he determined it was indeed the mark of leprosy, they had to tear out the walls. In some cases, the entire house had to be destroyed.

Note in Leviticus 14:36 that God orders the priest to command that the house be emptied. You see, to the Jews, their homes are little sanctuaries for God. All their furniture is chosen with God in mind and is blessed or made holy before God. Deuteronomy 20:5:

And the officers shall speak unto the people, saying, What man [is there] that hath built a new house, and hath not dedicated it? let him go and return to his house, lest he die in the battle, and another man dedicate it.

The Jews are to dedicate their homes to God. They do this by attaching a mezuzah to their door post and reciting the blessing:

Baruch atah Adonai Eloheinu melekch ha'olam, asher qideshanu bemitzvotav vetzivanu Blessed are you, Lord our God, King of the Uni-

*verse, who sanctified us with his mitzvot and commanded us to affix a
mezuzah.*

The Talmud teaches that the mezuzah helps the Jewish family to remember
that the true owner of their house is the Master of the Universe and that
they and their belongings are merely guests in His world. It is further written in the Talmud: "(God declares) If a man affixes a mezuzah, did I not give
him the house?"

The reason the priest allowed all the contents or furnishing to be removed
from the house before he examined the house for the mark of *tzara'at* was
that all the furnishings owned by the new tenants were dedicated to God.
The word dedicated in Hebrew is *chanak,* which means to dedicate, con-
secrate, or to make holy. God considered the contents of one's home to be
holy, that is, to be dedicated to God. What this means is that whatever God
gives us in this world belongs to Him; it is on loan from Him.

I remember a man in our church that I grew up in who was quite wealthy,
at least by the standards of the other people in the church. He was a building contractor who not only built commercial buildings, homes but also
churches. My mother was a trustee in our church for a long time, and one
day I happened to notice the financial books open on our dining room
table, and I saw the amount this man gave to the church in one year; it was
staggering and three to four times more than the total amounts given by
others on that page. This was on top of the money he gave to missions, to
our church camp, and the write-offs he made to many of the churches he
built. He was a man who most likely lived on 10% and gave God 90%.

His one big luxury was to purchase a new car every year, a Lincoln Continental. He did this because he really put the mileage on a car as his normal
workday was visiting his building sites, making estimates, and driving potential clients around. So, he would wear a car out every year. I overheard
him speaking with my father one day about his new car, and he said: "You
know, I paid as much for this car as I would have paid for a new Cadillac."
In that day, that was the top luxury car that one could own in this country.
He said that the Cadillac was of excellent quality, and he would prefer that
over his Lincoln just because it was a better-performing vehicle. But he
could not purchase one because other Christians would be offended that he
was purchasing such luxury rather than using that extra money he would
save with a lesser vehicle for the Lord's work. The fact he purchased a Lin-

coln was acceptable to Christians even though he paid as much for that as a Cadillac.

The point is, to that man, this Lincoln Continental, his home, his furniture, and all he possessed was holy to God. He recognized that it belonged to God and that it was only on loan to him. I take this a little further. God created his soul to be a soul for a person of means. His soul was created to be wealthy because it was a soul that was a giving soul, a soul that would use whatever was given to him by God, would be used for God. He prayed over his family, his home, his car, his furniture, and all he owned and *eucharistie, eulogesteo, shavach, 'avodi, barak* it, that is blessed it or made it holy.

There is nothing wrong with owning stuff. God created you to enjoy stuff. The problem with owning stuff is when you do not make it *eucharistie, eulogesteo, shavach, 'avodi, barak,* holy to God. You can own a wide flat-screen TV that covers your wall, and God will be pleased if you enjoy it. However, if you do not make it holy to God and use it to watch programming that is not honoring or in harmony with God, then you are misusing something that God loaned to you. You may have the wealth to afford a fancy luxury car which is clearly ok with God and matches your soul as God created it. You have a reason for a luxury car of good quality to carry out the work of God as this contractor did. However, if you start to show it off to boast of your wealth, then you have just made that possession of God unholy.

I read about a famous television preacher who purchased a new private Jet, his reason was that he could not fly commercial airlines as demons ride in such vehicles, and he could not travel to a speaking gig and be properly and spiritually prepared after traveling is such a vehicle, he had to have private transportation. Ah, the mockery that followed such a statement. I, too, joined in on the mockery. Yet, deep in my spirit, I felt a rebuke by God for taking pleasure in such mockery. It was almost like God was telling me: "I created this preacher's soul to be a man of wealth. His soul is compatible with this type of vehicle. Who are you to question his motives? He is only being what I created his soul to be. I created your soul to drive around in an old broken-down car, and that satisfies your soul. Every soul is created different and unique. Let me be the judge in what is holy and not holy." In other words, a brand-new private jet can be holy unto the Lord; it is not for us to judge. We need to be sure that what God has given to us has been made holy unto Him.

You see, table grace is nothing more than your soul reaffirming its creation and what it was created to be, which includes something that consumes food and even that is provided by the God who created your soul. We need to constantly reaffirm that simple message.

18. PRAYER OF PETITION

Genesis 48:22: "Moreover I have given to thee one portion above thy brethren, which I took out of the hand of the Amorite with my sword and with my bow."

I found something interesting when reading this verse in the Jewish Onkelos Targum. The Onkelos Targum is the primary Jewish Aramaic targum of the Torah or the first five books of the Bible. A targum was originally a spoken translation of the Hebrew Bible. A professional translator would give the Torah in the common language of the listeners. This became necessary near the end of the first century BC about the time Jesus walked the earth. At that time, the common language was Aramaic, and Hebrew was used for little more than schooling and worship. It was more of a ceremonial language like Latin in the Catholic church. What makes the Targums important is that the translator frequently expanded his translation with paraphrases, explanations, and examples so that it became like a sermon.

Writing down the targum was initially prohibited, but some targumitic writings did appear about the time of Jesus. Like our paraphrases today, they were not considered authoritative. Today the common understanding of a targum is a written Aramaic translation of the Old Testament which reflects the Midrashic interpretation of the Old Testament. Today they are a source of textual criticism and give us a sort of microscopic look into the Jewish thought of the first century, the era of Jesus, the disciples, the Apostle Paul, and the early church.

The Targum Onkelos of Genesis 48:22 gives us such insight into first-century Jewish thought that it helps shed some light on the concept of prayer. Before Jacob died, he gave a blessing to Joseph's two sons, Ephraim and Manasseh. That blessing was to bequeath to Ephraim and Manasseh a portion of land (Shechem) that Jacob took from the Amorites with *his sword and his bow.*

Genesis 33:19 tells us: *"And he bought a parcel of a field, where he had spread his tent, at the hand of the children of Hamor, Shechem's father, for an hundred pieces of money."* There is no record in Scripture that Jacob fought for this land with swords and bows and arrows. The Scriptural reference is that he purchased the land. The Midrash talks about a battle between Jacob and the Amorites who tried to take the land from Jacob, but the only record in the Bible we have of such an attempt and resulting battle in Scripture is in Genesis 48:22. Did such a battle take place? We do not know for sure, but the Targum Onkelos gives us a hint.

Now in Hebrew, the word bow is *qesheth,* which is an archer's bow used for hunting or warfare. So, in every modern English translation, we look at *qesheth,* and we correctly put in the English word bow. However, in our modern paraphrase versions, like the Contemporary English Version, they do what the translators of the targums did, and that is to paraphrase. That is not to give the exact word-for-word translation but the thought of the writer of the passage that is reflected in our modern-day English. Hence, since we are not sure of a bloody battle to place to capture the land, they translate this verse as *"Meanwhile, I'm giving you the hillside I captured from the Amorites."* It says nothing about a sword or bow; that is because there is no indication that this land was really captured by Jacob through the use of a bow and arrows. Maybe some other method was used to capture this land. Bow and arrows could be just a metaphor; we are not sure, so this paraphrase considers this and simply say it was captured by Jacob. In truth, the real capture was not through swords and bows but through the power of God.

Now why do we question whether or not Jacob captured this territory using swords and bows and arrows? Because the first-century targum says something a little different, which hints that swords and bows are really a metaphor. Not to say that God did not use swords and bows, but we need to understand it was God and not the swords and bows that captured the land. What the targum says is that the land was captured using *tsali* and *ba'i*. Both of these words are words for prayer in the Aramaic. *Tsali* is a prayer of dedication and devotion, and *ba'i* is a prayer of petition or request.

In other words, Jacob may have used a sword or bow and arrows to either fight or frighten off the Amorites, but the first-century Jews knew and understood that what Jacob meant and what was heard in the ears of Joseph and his sons was that he captured the land through his devotion to prayer and his prayers of petition to God.

Keeping in mind that the basic idea of prayer is an attachment to God, a notch in the tent peg that keeps us grounded in God. We can see that Jacob was not a man of war but a man who attached himself to God and found victory in his attachment to God.

Let's take this a little bit further. How is an archer's bow like prayer? Why is an archer's bow used as a metaphor for prayer, particularly a prayer of petition? Just like a bow, the more a person draws the bowstring to himself, the further the arrow flies. So it is with prayer; the deeper you draw your attachment to God into your heart, the higher it ascends, or the deeper into the heart of God your prayer request will descend.

It is interesting that the emphasis is not so much on your aim as it is on the depth that the bow string is drawn into one's heart. We aim for a lot of things when we draw that bowstring of prayer into our hearts. Perhaps we are praying for a new job that doubles our present salary with the hope of increasing our tithe to help the church and missionaries. As that bow is drawn further and further into our hearts, the real prayer, the prayer from our heart and the heart of God, is being touched, and that is not for greater wealth to finance a vacation, new car, and other luxuries but buried deep in our heart is the desire to give more to the church and missions and that is the prayer that is revealed as you pull that bow string tighter. You might not get the wealth for luxury, but your assets may become very valuable at the time you leave this earth, and it would increase your gift to the church and missionaries. That would likely be in the heart of God and likely create a pure prayer.

Jacob captured the land from the Amorites because that was what was in the heart of God, and it was in the heart of God that Joseph's sons who were yet born would inherit this land. Many times, our prayers, prayers from our heart, may not find their complete fulfillment until long after we have left this earth, as with Jacob.

19. PRAYER OF INTROSPECTION

Isaiah 16:3: "Take counsel, execute judgment; make thy shadow as the night in the midst of the noonday; hide the outcasts; bewray not him that wandereth."

The context of this verse is where the ambassadors of Moab have presented themselves before the rulers of Judah and encouraged them to take counsel and execute judgment. What is curious is the word that is used for judgment, and clearly, the context calls for the English word judgment is not the normal or common Hebrew word for judgment which is *shaphat*. Instead, the word that is used is *pelilah*. *Pelilah* is a word used to describe a process of introspection. It is interesting that *pelilah* comes from the same root word for prayer or *palal*.

Indeed, prayer is a time for inner reflection. If you think about it, if you live a life of prayer, you are not constantly asking for God to give you things or to help you out in the circumstances. Most of your time is spent just talking things over with God.

People who have watched the movie or seen the play Fiddler on the Roof often comment on the relationship the main character, Tevye, had with God and how he just talked with God as a friend would talk with a friend. For instance, in one scene, we find him not in a synagogue, not wearing a talit over his head, nor reciting some memorized prayer. Instead, he is just talking with God in his barn: "Dear Lord, you make many, many poor people. I realize, of course, it's no great shame to be poor. But it's no great honor either. Would it be so terrible if I had just a small fortune?" He is not asking

God to be rich, and he is not even complaining to God that he is not rich. He is just simply talking it over with God. He is in the process of introspection, of making some sort of judgment with regard to his circumstances, and he has chosen to include God in this time of introspection. He realizes that God created him to be what he is, just a poor milkman eking out an existence, living his life the best way he can to fulfill whatever mission it is that God sent him into the world to accomplish.

If I use myself as an example, I would daresay that the majority of my prayers are introspection, having a conversation with God. Just talking things over with God. In *pelilah* prayers, we are reflecting on what we truly want in life, the direction we are heading, and just how far along we are in our journey through life. As a believer in God, we just naturally want to include God in this time of introspection. Many times, the answer to our dilemmas comes from just talking things out with God. There is no angel appearing to give us direction, there is no voice coming out of heaven, there is just that simple knowing that God is either pleased with our journey or not, and if He is not, we seek to change direction and follow a path that He is pleased with.

Thomas Merton was a Trappist monk at the Abbey of Gethsemani, a gifted writer, philosopher, and theologian who lived in silence for much of his life. This is the same monastery that I go to for my spiritual retreat, where I live in silence for a week. He wrote: "People may spend their whole lives climbing the ladder of success only to find once they reach the top, that the ladder is leaning against the wrong wall."

From the many hours during my silent retreats at the monastery, I would sit and just talk with Jesus about my life, the direction I was going, and what I really wanted to accomplish with my life. Many times, during my prayers of *pelilah,* I discovered that I had placed my ladder against the wrong wall, and when I returned from my journey into silence, I placed my ladder against a wall that I knew would bring God pleasure. So many decisions I make in life are meant to bring me pleasure, only to discover I have no pleasure in those decisions, that the real pleasure I feel is to feel the pleasure of God.

I have discovered that when I neglect my prayers of *pelilah,* I find myself feeding my soul and nourishing my soul with things that strengthen my own ego, and before long, my prayers are basically prayers of petitions. Then after a while, it seems like the only time I approach God would be like the old boy from down South who would say: "You just come with a handful of gimmie and a mouthful of much obliged." I end up saying what I want and not what God wants, even though my heart cries out for what God wants.

You know God doesn't listen to our petitions; He knows what our needs are even before we ask. He does not sit on His throne with his chin in his hand, patiently listening to us as we rattle on and on with our requests. Matthew 6:7-8:

> *But when ye pray, use not vain repetitions, as the heathen do: for they think that they shall be heard for their much speaking. (8) Be not ye therefore like unto them: for your Father knoweth what things ye have need of, before ye ask him.*

Prayer is not communicating to God information that He does not already know. God doesn't need our prayers; we need them. The moment someone asks me to pray for them, it is done, accomplished. My prayer is lifted up to God. However, I need to take that person's hand and speak the words of his prayer, maybe filled with a lot of thees and thous just so he gets a spiritual feel, but God is already on the road to answering that prayer, in fact, He has answered it before I even get to my "amen."

In any relationship, there is the need for communication. Without communication, that relationship will die. So too with God, we need to communicate with Him, not that He needs to hear us out, but we need to hear ourselves seeking Him, and we need to search out our hearts and let God shine a light on what He sees, but we do not see unless we take the time to see what that Light is revealing.

20. PLAYING WITH GOD

II Samuel 6:14, 21: "And David danced before the Lord with all his might."(21) And David said unto Michal, [It was] before the LORD, which chose me before thy father, and before all his house, to appoint me ruler over the people of the LORD, over Israel: therefore will I celebrate before the LORD.

I've watched a number of these phony movies about King David, and I am always disappointed when they show the scene of David dancing before the Ark of the Covenant. It is usually portrayed as a well-choreographed dance set to some fine music. With the words I find in the Hebrew, I doubt that this was a well-rehearsed exercise. So, what was this dance? Was it jumping around in a frenzy? Was this a choreographed dance, or was it spontaneous? Poor David has sure taken a lot of heat over this from many Christians. However, we tend to miss something very important in this verse, which would also serve as a very important lesson for us.

David danced *before* the Lord. The Hebrew word used for *before* is *lipeni*. This is often used as a preposition, but it can also be used as an adjective. As a preposition, it would simply mean that David danced before God. But as an adjective, it would mean that David danced in God's presence. Actually, it would be more correct to say that David danced with God.

Come on, I mean, really? When you are in a worship service worshipping God, saying all sorts of praisallujahs and telling Him how wonderful He is, what do you think God is doing? Is He sitting up on His throne, looking down, taking it all in, saying: "Hey angels, come over here a minute. Listen to this guy called Chaim Bentorah and what he is saying. My word, but he really knows what he is talking about, telling me how wonderful and marvelous I am. Yep, I sure am. I tell ya, pay attention to that Chaim Bentorah fellow; he sure can praise. While you're at it, put Him down for a blessing; see that his next book is a best seller." Is God that insecure that He needs our constant praise to reassure Himself that He is awesome? Or that he won't release a blessing unless we tell Him how wonderful He is?

I read in the Talmud something very interesting. That preposition for before should really read as "with." Thus, this should read that David danced with God, not before God. He wasn't dancing to get his Father's hugs, which he already had. He was dancing with his Heavenly Father out of pure joy, and the Father was there before the Ark of the Covenant, dancing with David. Note the Hebrew word for dance that is used here is *karar*. The common word for *dance* in Hebrew is *mawkhole*, but that is not used here. In fact, *karar* is used only two times in the Hebrew Bible, both in this passage. In extra-Biblical sources, *karar* does not mean to dance at all; it means to *spin around like a top*. Spinning in a circle was a form of worship mostly practiced by children in ancient times.

I was in a worship service once, and I saw a little three or four-year-old girl rush out into the church aisle and begin to spin in a circle, just spinning around in pure joy. In my spirit, I saw Jesus smiling and laughing, and He was spinning this little child around just to delight her.

Indeed, even today in the Middle East, the Mevlevy of the Sufi order of Islam perform a sema by spinning around in a circle. They are known as Whirling Dervishes (a Dervish is an initiate of the Suri Path). They believe that spinning around in a circle is symbolic of throwing off your ego.

David did this spin in *becal 'oz—in full power*. The pronoun *his* is not there in the Hebrew. In fact, *karar,* in its Semitic root, means one who is possessed. My guess is that this full might *becal 'oz* was spinning him around laughing and playing like I imagined that little girl was spinning around just possessed with the presence of God.

In verse 20, we learn David's wife, Michal, was upset with him because he danced naked. The word *naked or uncovered,* however, is the word *nigelah* in Hebrew. This word is rarely used for naked. Its primary focus is to *open up or reveal a secret*. In its Semitic root, it has the idea of a return to a beginning. David was supposed to be the spiritual head honcho of Israel, a king, a pastor, a Christian leader. There he was, spinning around like a little child, returning to his beginning as a child. How could people have confidence in a spiritual leader who acts like a child? What was David's reply? In verse 21, he tells his wife that it was with God; therefore, I *sichaketi* with God. Most of our modern translations render *sichaketi* as celebrate. But that is a rare usage of this word. The primary use of the word is the English word "playing."

Of course, most translators abhor the idea of playing with God, so they stretch out the meaning to be celebrate. I say it we use play. Jesus just joins in with our worship, singing and dancing with us, having fun, and playing with us as friends play with friends. Do you and God ever play together, do you ever dance together, do you spin in circles together? I wonder what Jesus really meant when he gathered children around Him and said that unless you become like little children, you cannot enter the kingdom of God. I think it meant more than just the faith of a child; I think it also meant that God likes to play with his children like any parent would. Somehow, I think that during that worship service with that little girl spinning in a circle, as people were reciting their Bless you and praise you Lords, Jesus grabbed that little girl's hand and said: "Come on, little one, I've heard enough, let's dance."

Sometimes our prayer time can be what David experienced, simply a play time like a little child.

21. PRAYER AS A SACRIFICE

Ezekiel 1:10,13: "As for the likeness of their faces, each had the face of a man; each of the four had the face of a lion on the right side, each of the four had the face of an ox on the left side, and each of the four had the face of an eagle. (13) As for the likeness of the living creatures, their appearance was like burning coals of fire, like the appearance of torches going back and forth among the living creatures. The fire was bright, and out of the fire went lightning.

We really do not spend much time reading the book of Ezekiel because there is so much cryptic language in this book. Ezekiel 1 is one such chapter. Commentators have waxed lyrical about the significance of these visions of Ezekiel, and there are many interpretations thereof. Since there are so many different interpretations, I would like to offer my own personal interpretation. I find that deep within Jewish mystical works; there are some interesting insights which I do not discount but cannot help but put a Christian spin on such insights. Now to be sure, I do not read the Zohar to seek any spiritual benefit; I only do it to practice my study of Aramaic. The Aramaic of the Zohar is a bit different than Talmudic Aramaic and the Aramaic of the Targum, so I do find it necessary to get a feel of the Aramaic of the Zohar. I can't say I even have an elementary understanding of the esoteric nature of the Zohar, and personally, I don't seek an understanding of the Zohar. I have other mountains to climb. I just want to expand what little skills I have with the Aramaic. With that said, I did run across something interesting that I could not help but make a spiritual application. As this is a personal view, I only offer it for your consideration.

For instance, in the Talmud in Berachot 26b, I read that "Prayers were instituted based upon the daily offerings sacrificed in the Holy Temple." Now since there is no longer a Temple or altar to offer sacrifices, the sages established daily prayers to take the place of the sacrifices. That really started my creative juices to flow when I started to consider our prayers as sacrifices. But what does the slaughter and burning of innocent animals have to do with prayer?

This is where I found something interesting in the Zohar, which is a Jewish mystical book. Now if that word "mystical" troubles you, I suggest you read no further. However, for me personally, the idea of mystical is not Micky Mouse wearing a pointed hat and waving a magic wand. The fundamental idea of mysticism, in the context that I use this word, is believing that there is a God who hears our prayers, who answers our prayers, and that we have a personal relationship with this God. I mean, how much more mystical can you get than saying that you believe there is a God you cannot see who created the universe, who lives inside of you, loves you, and that you are actually carrying on conversations with this unseen God?

So, what I found interesting in the Zohar is that it teaches that during the first Temple, a fire would descend from heaven to consume the sacrifice. Well, the Bible itself does teach that. What is interesting, however, is the Jewish teachers said the fire came in the form of a "lion." Perhaps in my interpretation, I should capitalize the word "Lion" like the Lion of Judah. It is from Ezekiel 1:13 that these teachers associate fire with the lion. The ox is associated with the physical body, physical desires and wants of the human. The Lion is pictured as the fire of redemption, which devours these human desires.

Now keep in mind that I am applying a Christian interpretation here; this is not the Jewish interpretation. When the fire in the form of the Lion devoured the ox, which represents the desires of the human physical soul, the energy, or shall we say from a Christian standpoint, the sins of the human, are consumed by the fire of God and absorbed by His Son Jesus Christ. As we teach, Jesus Christ took all those sins to the Cross, where they were burned away by the shedding of His blood. You see, the Lion (Jesus Christ) is the true source of the souls of humankind as it was God who breathed the *neshamah,* the eternal soul, into the human.

Let me just offer here that the sacrifice of prayer is a prayer for the redemption of our sins. So long as we live in this human body, represented by the ox, we are going to sin. There is a natural battle between our redeemed soul and our physical body. My grandfather used to tell the story of a Native American who became a Christian, and when asked what it was like, he said it was like two dogs inside of him who were constantly fighting, one good and one evil. When asked which one wins, he said, "Whichever one I feed the most." As long as we live in the human body, represented by the ox, we will feed the ox more than the redeemed soul, which I picture as the eagle. Hence, we must, through prayer, confess those sins, and when we do, the Lion of Judah comes as a fire to consume the sins of the ox.

So, why a Lion, ox, and eagle? The word lion in Hebrew is *'arah* which is a powerful leader, the leader among all leaders. We have heard that the lion is the king among the animals or the King of the Jungle. Throughout history, including ancient history, the lion has always been respected as the king among all animals. One reason is because of its raw power and strength. Lions do not fear any animals, but they do have enemies. Its worst enemy is the hyena and jackal. The hyenas and jackals are much smaller animals and much less powerful than the lion. They eat the same food as the lion and will steal the lion's food when the lion is not looking. They let the lion do all the work, hunting and capturing its prey, and then the hyena comes along and steals his food. What better picture of Jesus, the Lion of Judah, who fights against the enemy, an enemy who is weaker and trying to steal His food? That food is represented by the ox, our physical body, which is destroying our *neshamah* - soul.

The word for ox in Hebrew is *shur* which has the idea of blocking one's vision. Our physical bodies, our ox, are constantly blocking our spiritual vision. All we see is this natural world and what we want in this physical realm. We place our natural desires ahead of our spiritual desires, and the enemy uses that to cause us to sin. Finally, when Jesus, the Lion of Judah, devours the ox, the natural physical desires, it releases our eagle. The word eagle is *nesher* in Hebrew. *Nesher* has two possible root words *nasar* and *nashar*. *Nasar* is the idea of ripping and tearing apart, and *nesher* is a word for protection, freedom from fear. When sin has been ripped away from us and burned in the spiritual fire on the altar, our souls or *neshamah* are then freed, for we are protected from the penalty of our sin.

But note what I mentioned earlier that when the temple was destroyed, the Jews could no longer offer a sacrifice. So today, prayer takes the place of sacrifice. We should never forget the need to daily offering a sacrificial prayer.

But let's examine this a little further in Exodus 40:30-31: "*He set the laver between the tabernacle of meeting and the altar, and put water there for washing; (31) and Moses, Aaron, and his sons would wash their hands and their feet with water from it.*

John 13:5-8:

> *After that he poureth water into a bason, and began to wash the disciples' feet, and to wipe them with the towel wherewith he was girded. (7) Jesus answered and said unto him, What I do thou knowest not now; but thou shalt know hereafter. (8) Peter saith unto him, Thou shalt never wash my feet. Jesus answered him, If I wash thee not, thou hast no part with me.*

Moses, Aaron, and Aaron's sons were commanded to wash their hands and feet before entering the temple to perform the service of the sacrifice. At other times they were only required to wash their hands. Why are they now required to wash their feet and their hands?

I read something in the *Sefer Avoda Biat Hamikdash* (Order of service (for the) tabernacle/temple). This may shed some deeper understanding of the events of John 13 when Jesus washed his disciple's feet. Jesus indicated that this was a ceremony to be performed by his disciples to show their servitude and humility. But Jesus also hinted at something even deeper when He went to wash Peter's feet, and he objected. Jesus's response was rather curious. He told Peter that there was something that he did not yet understand. Jesus had to point out to him that if he did not allow Him to wash his feet, Peter would have no part of him. The expression of having "no part" is a Hebraic expression related to an inheritance. Obviously, Jesus was doing more than performing a cultural ritual; He was giving a deeper spiritual lesson.

In the *Biat Hamikkdash chapter 5,* we learn that there are two levels of sanctity. The first level of sanctity is purity. The second level is holiness. Washing of the feet was the removal of impurities and becoming pure. Yet, that was not enough for the priest to achieve sanctity. To be truly sanctified, one needs to achieve holiness. Holiness can only come after one is purified. If one is purified, there would be no need to wash the feet; one just needs to wash their hands. Even today, Orthodox Jews will wash their hands before prayer but not their feet. They believe they live in that first level of sanctity, but to pray, they must be holy, and hence they wash their hands as a sign of holiness, washing away impurities.

To the Jew, as long as there was a temple, you could achieve holiness as a sacrifice was offered in the temple to provide the cleansing of sin. However, after the sacrifice, the High Priest would offer up incense from the altar of incense. There were only two items in the temple that never became impure, the brazen altar where the sacrifice was made and the altar of incense where prayers were made. When the temple was destroyed, and no sacrifice could be offered, prayer took the place of sacrifice.

At the time Jesus was washing his disciples' feet, the temple still stood, and sacrifices were offered. However, Jesus was going to be that sacrifice which Peter did not yet understand. The ritual of washing the disciples' feet had a deeply spiritual significance. The word wash in Hebrew is *rachatz* which means to wash thoroughly, immerse in a liquid. But it also means to make and maintain purity in a spiritual sense. The word is closely related to *racham*, the pure love of God. To wash – *rachatz* one's hands would bring one to the second level of sanctification, that is, to be cleansed of impurities which would reveal the *racham* love of God.

The hands of Jesus washed the feet of the disciples. The hands of Jesus were pure, and the purity of the hands of Jesus washing his disciples' feet made them holy, for it is the purity of the hands that bring holiness in Jewish thought. Jesus was demonstrating that by washing the disciple's feet, He would remove the impurities to make them pure to bring them into holiness, that second level of sanctity. If he were not allowed to wash that is *rachatz* the feet of Peter, Peter would never be holy and hence would not be sanctified and thus would not inherit the Kingdom of God.

There is this delightful elderly woman; we will call her Gloria, who lives in a senior citizen's apartment building. She is a real servant of God and loves God with all her heart, soul, and might. Yet, she is still human. She told the story of another woman who lives in an apartment down the hall from her. She was a real sour, prune-faced bitty of a woman who seemed to hate Gloria for no other reason than she was always so happy and talking about the Lord. She started gossiping to the other residents that Gloria stole some of her personal belongings when she visited her apartment. She warned others to beware of inviting Gloria into their apartment as all her good Christian behavior was just an excuse to case out their apartment and seek an opportunity to steal from them.

When Gloria learned of this, she confronted this woman and sort of lost her sanctification. She declared that she would never speak to this woman nor have anything to do with her. She also shared a few other little unChristian words. She felt bad about her behavior but was unrepentant, as she felt this woman deserved it and more.

One day she got a call from this very woman who was in tears. She pleaded with Gloria to come to her apartment and help her remove some bandages. This woman needed to change these bandages, and no one was willing to help her. Gloria found herself whispering to God: "No, no, no!" But she gave in, not out of any love but just pity.

When she entered this woman's apartment, she was horrified to see her feet covered with bandages soaked in blood. She had these bleeding ulcers on her feet, and the bandages should have been changed days earlier. Gloria immediately grabbed a basin of warm water and soaked off the bandages. The woman's feet were covered with sores, and Gloria had no choice but to rachatz – wash these sores on her feet and apply fresh bandages. As she was cleansing these sores, she was repeating over and over in her mind: "Lord, why are you making do this for this woman? Why do I have to wash her feet?" Then it hit her: "I'm washing her feet!" Like the woman in Luke 7:36-50 who washed Jesus's feet with her tears, Gloria wept while washing this woman's feet, confessing her bitterness to God and this woman, asking for forgiveness.

I believe both women entered into qodesh—holiness by the washing—*rachatz* of the feet. They became *palal*, attached to God. That little ceremony for Gloria was really a prayer. Prayer does indeed come in many shapes, forms, and sizes.

22. ONE SIZE FITS ALL

Habakkuk 1:2: "O Lord, how long shall I cry, and thou wilt not hear!
Even cry out unto thee of violence, and thou wilt not save!"

Have you ever prayed for something, and it seems that God never gets around to answering that prayer? I would daresay that all of us have had that experience, probably more than we will admit. You have to appreciate Habakkuk's honesty; at least he admits that God does not hear his cry. Poor Habakkuk had been fasting, praying, and pleading with God for an answer to a prayer, and it seemed to never come. I can sure relate to old Habakkuk; for years, I have been praying for something; I have fasted and pleaded with God. I have even resorted to non-Biblical approaches like trying to bargain with God or bribe God with promises of increased offerings and church attendance.

What is very disconcerting is my prayer is pretty selfish, whereas Habakkuk's prayer was more for others than himself, that God would do something about the violence in Israel. Unlike me, whose prayer concerns my own gizzard, Habakkuk's prayer was purely unselfish; he was praying for his nation and his people. If God could not get around to answering Habakkuk's noble unselfish prayer, what chance have I got with my petty little "me first" prayer?

Then again, does God keep some sort of priority checklist to determine at what point He will get around to answering a prayer? Does it really matter if your prayer is selfish or unselfish? Is God more inclined to answer a prayer if it is unselfish over a selfish prayer? Do not all prayers carry a bit of selfishness in them? I see people gathering together in great numbers to pray for our nation. They, like Habakkuk, pray for our nation and pray about the violence they are seeing. They weep, fast, and cry out to God because of the violence they are seeing in our nation. What motivates such an outcry? We have to admit that many, not all, but many of these prayers are born out of personal fear that they will be affected personally by this violence—that maybe our nation will collapse economically and governmentally, maybe even to the point where we lose our religious freedom.

The English word violence is pretty harsh. I believe it is a poor choice of word for the Hebrew word that is used, which is *chaman*. But in some ways, it is not. This word has an extremely broad usage. This is a word that can speak volumes. This word expresses the idea of wealth or pleasure that is obtained through violence, oppression, theft, etc. It includes predatory lending, Ponzi schemes, and corrupt businessmen who put others out of business to enhance their own. It includes corrupt means of government to obtain funds, like allowing a lottery to move beyond a game to an act of desperation among people. It even includes those who get abortions so they can pursue their own selfish lifestyles. Ultimately, it carries out the idea of enhancing your own power, wealth, and/or pleasure at the expense of another person. *Chaman* even involves little things like overcharging for your services or a product. Yes, even selling a used car for its market value but not telling the buyer it needs a new transmission. And even that subtle difference of asking for a donation from someone and telling them rather than reminding them that God will (rather than saying may) bless them in a financial way for that donation. Using God's blessing as a tool to enhance your own power or wealth base, like giving an offering to get more from God rather than giving out of a sacrificial heart of love. That is what is encompassed in that word *chaman,* which we translate as violence. If you have a better English word to plug in here, I am open to it. Habakkuk's cry is not much different from our cry against the *chaman* we are experiencing today, and as much as we cry out, the *chaman* just continues.

The simple fact is that God hears all our prayers and answers all our prayers, no matter what degree of selfishness is behind that prayer or even if they are devoid of selfishness. Ultimately, it comes down to that little phrase in Lord's prayer that we often forget to add to our prayers: "Thy will be done on earth as it is in heaven."

There is something more to Habakkuk's prayers which is "God do something." Habakkuk cries to God in verse 2, asking *why* He allows all this to go on. That is something I do not do when my prayer goes on answered is to ask God, "Why?" Maybe I don't ask because I am a little less confident of receiving an answer to a question than I am of an answer to a need. Getting an answer to a need can just suddenly appear. I need a new computer, and voila, things come together, and I have a new computer, praisealleuia. Yet, to get a direct answer to a question from God means something much more personal, and is my relationship with God so personal that I will actually hear Him give me an answer?

Habakkuk was so close to God that he could hear an answer, and when he got his answer to the question, why. Maybe we don't need to have a vision, dream, or angelic vision to get a direct answer to why God did not answer our prayer. Perhaps the answer is found in Scripture itself. We have such an answer in Habakkuk. Habakkuk understood the answer to his first prayer was found in the answer to his second prayer as to why it seemed like God was not doing something about the *chaman* or violence.

God explains to Habakkuk that He was preparing a coming judgment to fall on the nation. There is an old saying that I get sick of hearing, but I have to admit it is true; "Be careful what you pray for." Habakkuk sort of regretted asking God, "Why do you not answer?" God tells Habakkuk that not only has He answered the prayer, but just how He was going to deal with this *chaman*. He was preparing the Babylonians to overpower the nation; they would kill, rape, steal, plunder, and destroy the nation. Many would die, all would be destitute, and they would starve and be homeless. Their nation, one of the most powerful and wealthiest nations in the world, would be reduced overnight into a nation like a third-world nation.

That wasn't the answer Habakkuk wanted. That is not the answer that those who are praying for our nation would want. He, like us, expected God to send a great revival in the land, and there would be singing and dancing, and everyone would be secure and happy, and all that evil *chaman* would end. Being reduced to poverty and third-world nation status did not seem to be the answer he was looking for. Yet revival would come, just not quite the way Habakkuk wanted.

But the question goes even deeper. Why should the just and righteous have to suffer along with the *chaman* makers? I watch videos of Christians who are earnestly praying for our nation. Usually, these prayer meetings are accompanied by some prophet who gives a glowing prophecy of deliverance and revival. What if God's response is like the one Habakkuk got? Well, for one thing, the live stream feed would quickly be ended if someone were to offer such a prophecy. We just don't want to hear it. But, if such a prophecy were given, would we not ask the same question? "We are the faithful; we prayed for this nation; why do we have to suffer along with the *chaman* makers?" God tells Habakkuk in 2:4: "But the just shall live by faith." What kind of answer is that? Faith in what? Like it or not, God knows us better than we know ourselves, and we must have faith that whatever He does will be for our benefit. We want our faith to keep us out of trouble. Yet, if we read further in the Book of Habakkuk, we see that he comes to a realization of what they just must have their faith in, and that is found in chapter 3, verses 17-18:

Although the fig tree will not blossom, neither will there be fruit on the vines; the labor of the olive will fail, and the fields will yield no food, the flock will be cut off from the fold, and there will be no herd in the stalls: **still I will be able to rejoice in the Lord, I will joy in the God of my salvation.**

If God repeats history upon our nation and the glowing prophecies of our nation's enemies being overthrown and peace and love do not come to rule our land, does it mean that God has not heard our prayers and answered them? Actually, God is telling Habakkuk that there is a one size fits all answer to all our prayers, whether it be my selfish little prayer to our prayers for our nation. It is the assurance that we will rejoice, no matter what happens, no matter what the outcome. If we break down every prayer we pray, the vast majority of those prayers that contain a selfish motive can be defined as a prayer to just be happy, to be able to rejoice. Sometimes we think we know better than God what it takes for us to be happy and rejoice.

I recall the story of a man who overheard his cleaning lady pray to God as she was cleaning the bathroom. She prayed: "Oh Lord, if I just had fifty dollars right now, I would be the most contented woman in the world. I would truly be happy and satisfied." Intrigue at the idea of seeing a contended and satisfied person, he went to his cleaner and told her he overheard her prayer and gave her the fifty dollars. Then when he walked out of the bathroom, he put his ear to the door and listened to her pray. Her prayer was: "Oh Lord, why didn't I say one hundred dollars."

The word rejoice is *'alaz* which means to be so full of joy that you are expressing it physically in a smile, a dance, a shout. Now that is really joy. God reminded Habakkuk that in the midst of poverty and desolation, the just will be happy. They will find joy in the God of their salvation. "Joy" is the Hebrew word *gayal* which means to move in a circle and tremble. You will be so filled with the joy of the Lord that you will spin like a top and actually tremble with joy.

I recall a pastor who was imprisoned in a communist country for just being a Christian. He lost everything that brought him happiness, his family, home, church, and financial security. Yet, he said while he was in solitary confinement, in a cold, dark cell, the Lord's presence so filled him that he was dancing and singing to God out of pure joy. He even said sometimes he becomes nostalgic for those days in prison just to experience that overwhelming joy again. But God reminds him that He was just giving him what he needed at that time and moment. Once he was free and living a comfortable life, he did not need that intense joy that God was keeping for those special moments.

You see, maybe the reason we do not feel God answers our prayers is that He sees the very root or need behind our prayer, the longing for joy and happiness. God does not always hear the cry of our flesh but the cry of our heart, which is often two different things. The cry of our flesh may be for a new car, job, relationship, etc., but really, the cry of our heart may be just for simple joy and happiness, and God is ready to give it in abundance if we just realize that is what we really want and we look for it in Him.

No, God has not answered that prayer of mine, but then again, maybe he has, and I am just too stubborn to accept His answer. Yet, in those quiet moments when I am alone with Him, He fills me with such joy and peace that I find myself saying: "Ok, Lord, you don't need to answer my prayer; Your grace is sufficient; it is all I need. I don't need that selfish thing for which I have been praying because it could never bring the joy I feel with you at this moment.

23. POUR YOUR HEART OUT TO GOD

Psalm 62:8: *"Trust in him at all times; [ye] people, pour out your heart before him: God [is] a refuge for us. Selah."*

In I Samuel, we see the story of a woman named Hannah who was barren. Every year she would go to the temple and plead with God to give her a child. She prayed, wept, pleaded, and literally poured her out to God such that the High Priest accused her of being drunk. It is taught by many Jewish teachers that Hannah's prayer is really a model for Jewish prayer, and I would add, for Christian prayer as well. If prayer is palal, attaching ourselves to God, then we need to bond with God, and one way two people bond with each other is when they share the secrets of their hearts with each other and pour their hearts out to each other.

In 1902 Adelaide Pollard was hoping to go to Africa as a missionary but was unable to raise the funds needed to pay for her missionary venture. She became greatly discouraged. She had set her heart on being a missionary and just could not understand why God was not blessing her efforts to serve him in this capacity. She kept this inner pain to herself, but it was wearing her down. She so wanted to serve God as a missionary, had planned on it, trained for it, and now it appeared like she would have to head in another direction with her life. How could God not honor such a noble request?

She attended a prayer meeting where she heard an elderly woman pray: "It really doesn't matter what you do with us, Lord, just have your own way with our lives." God immediately led Pollard to Jeremiah 18:6: "O house of Israel, cannot I do with you as this potter? saith the LORD. Behold, as the clay [is] in the potter's hand, so [are] ye in mine hand, O house of Israel."

That night she went home and just wept before the Lord. She cried out all her disappointments, discouragements, rejections, and heartbreak, and then she began to pray a prayer that took on the form of a poem. After praying this prayer, she immediately wrote out the words that she prayed. Before long, music was added to these, and it became a classic hymn, one which many have sung at one time or another. I sang this song myself as a prayer to God when I was just a child, and I still pray that prayer today. That song/hymn is "Have Thine Own Way."

Every modern English translation I read renders Psalms 62:8 as *pour out your heart.* I don't think we need to expound too much on this to explain what it means to pour out your heart. Commentators give us a good example in I Samuel 1:13-15 with Hannah pouring out her heart to God. Yet, in this case, she merely spoke her heart. That word, spoken in Hebrew, is the word *debar* which is used to express the idea of speaking your heart. However, in Psalm 62:8, David is not saying to just speak your heart to God but to *shaphak* your heart to God. The word *shaphak* comes from an old Canaanite word for melting wax and pouring it into a mold. The word pour is not a wrong translation; it is just not a complete translation of this word. You need to melt and pour your heart out to God.

What does it mean to melt your heart? I think Miss Pollard knew what it meant. Her heart was solid, it was set on going to Africa as a missionary. It was as if the desires of her heart were set in stone. That stony heart had to be melted. Only when it is melted can God then begin to mold it into what He really wants to do with it.

What could be more noble than going to Africa as a missionary? Surely God would say: "Oy, what a dedicated spirit I have, why I must grant her request immediately. Rich man, I command you to give this saintly woman the funds to go to Africa." But that was not what God wanted. That is what she wanted. God had created her for something else, if for anything, to write the song "Have Thine Own Way," a song which would influence and melt the hearts of thousands, perhaps millions, this writer included. It is possible that song alone accomplished more than anything she could have done on the mission field. She wrote over 100 songs and taught at the Christian and Missionary Alliance School, training future missionaries. Through her work, she prepared hundreds of others to go to the mission field.

You know, for many of us, things just do not go the way we hoped or planned. As I look over the many years of my life since my graduation from seminary, I can only shake my head in despair, and I consider how so few things ever turned out as I had hoped or planned. Many times, like Adelaide Pollard, I fall before God weeping over my shattered hopes and plans. It is then that God reaches back into my childhood and brings out that old song, Have Thine Own Way. I begin singing that old hymn, and over and over, I sing those words melt me, mold me, use me. I ask God to melt my heart and then pour it into His mold to be what he wants it to be.

My father used to always keep reminding me as I shared with him my lofty plans for my future. "It doesn't matter what you do or what you accomplish; if He has your heart, that is all that matters." My father was just a milkman who loved Jesus with all his heart. He spent his time doing whatever he could in our church, from teaching Sunday School, working with the teenagers as a youth sponsor, and being an Awana Commander. The rest of his time was spent down in the rundown area of Chicago, ministering to the men on the streets outside the Bible Rescue Mission. It would not be the lofty great ideas I had for my life, but as I look upon it now, it was what the heart of God wanted for my father, and he allowed his heart to be *shaphak*, melted, and molded to God's heart. He ended up accomplishing more by the time he reached my age than I have ever accomplished. Perhaps that is why I am now on this journey to discover God's heart. Hopefully, when I discover God's heart, I will find myself planted firmly in His.

24. GOD'S PERFECT PRAYER

Matthew 6:9-13: "After this manner therefore pray ye: Our Father which art in heaven, Hallowed be thy name. (10) Thy kingdom come. Thy will be done in earth, as it is in heaven. (11) Give us this day our daily bread. (12) And forgive us our debts, as we forgive our debtors. (13) And lead us not into temptation, but deliver us from evil: For thine is the kingdom, and the power, and the glory, for ever. Amen.

I remember I had a Christian friend that I deeply respected as a man of God. He once told me that the perfect prayer was the "Our Father" or "Lord's Prayer," as we protestants call it. Indeed, it was given to us by Jesus, who said that when we pray, we are to pray like the prayer that He gave. This is the prayer that is prayed almost every Sunday in most churches and by many Christians every day. Did Jesus intend for us to recite this prayer word for word or just use it as a model?

First, before we start out, one needs to understand the mindset of a first-century Jewish Semite. This is so in conflict with our Western thinking that I feel it is necessary to express it. The Jewish mindset of that day, as it is today, is that all we have, even our very lives are on loan from God. "*The Lord gives and the Lord takes away, blessed be the name of the Lord." Job 1:21.* He just loans it all to us, and as a creditor, He can call for its return at any time. I saw a documentary of Israeli soldiers getting ready to go to battle. They stood before a rabbi to receive a blessing. They removed their helmets but not their kippah. That kippah was to remind themselves that even in battle, they were to remember that all they do, they do as unto God and that they are always in the presence of God. It reminds them of one other thing, even their very lives are on loan from God, and if they fall in battle, they are only returning their bodies to God, which were on loan to them. In Jewish thought, one does not die; they just leave their physical bodies behind and continue the life that God has given them in the spirit. When we enter a study of the Lord's Prayer, we must do it with this mindset.

One other mindset we need. Do you ever notice it is "*Our* Father," not "*My* Father?" Give *us* this day *our* daily bread" and not "give *me* this day *my* daily bread," "lead *us* not into temptation," and not "lead *me* into temptation?" Jews are taught that when they pray, they are to pray as a community and for the community. It may even be that the model of prayer we learn from the Lord's Prayer is to always pray as and for the community or fellowship of believers, whether we pray as a group or alone.

Next, let me point out something I will reference, and that is that the study of the Northern Dialect or Old Galilean Aramaic is relatively new. The Western Church has taken the position that the New Testament was written in Greek, and therefore Greek has been the language of choice for Seminaries and Bible Colleges down through the centuries.

I drove an Eastern Orthodox priest to the dentist on my disability bus the other day. He was educated in an Eastern Orthodox seminary in the Ukraine. I asked him if the Eastern Orthodox really believed the New Testament was written in Syriac (Aramaic), and he said that was true. I asked him if he studied Syriac, and he said no, only Greek. I asked why study Greek if they believe the New Testament was written in Syriac. He said that was a decision made by the powers in the church centuries ago. One reason is that there are far more Greek manuscripts than Aramaic. I asked why there were so few Aramaic manuscripts, and he said that Constantine destroyed all he could get his hands on. The libraries of Carthage were said to have carried many of the original Aramaic manuscripts, and these were burned to the ground in 146 BC by the Romans. The earliest Greek complete manuscript, Codex Sinaiticus and the Codex Vaticanus, are dated to the fourth century AD. The oldest complete manuscript of the Aramaic, Syriac Sinaitic, is also dated to the fourth Century AD, although there is a fragment that dates to 150 AD. However, there are about 5,800 manuscripts of the New Testament in Greek and only 350 manuscripts in Syriac.

Most scholars, particularly in the West, agree the New Testament was written in Greek. However, there is a growing number of scholars who are beginning to question this. All agree that Jesus and His disciples spoke a Northern Dialect of Aramaic, but there are scholars who believe the disciples were multi-lingual and spoke Greek as well. This is highly debated, especially as Josephus noted it was forbidden for many Jews to learn Greek as it was considered a pagan language.

So, what I am presenting in my study of the Lord's Prayer reflects my study of the prayer in Aramaic, and thus it does not have the Good Housekeeping Seal of Approval. I am sort of like the doctor selling his vitamins without FDA approval who hasn't yet been forced to put a warning notice on the label. But judge for yourself. I believe more and more information is coming out of Archaeological discoveries, particularly with the Dead Sea Scrolls, that are giving some credence to the Aramaic as the primary source. To be fair, the Syriac of the Peshitta, the standard Bible of the Eastern Orthodox and Aramaic text, is not identical to the Aramaic that Jesus spoke, although it is considered very close.

With regard to the Lord's Prayer, we find a number of problems in the Greek text which are easily resolved in the Aramaic text. For instance, the wording of the prayer is awkward in Greek, Latin, and English. Why does Jesus say, "Our Father who art in heaven," when He lives inside of us? Why does He say: "Lead us not into temptation" and "Give us this day our daily bread?" Does God really lead us into temptation? Why does Jesus say in Matthew 6:8 that the Father knows your need before you ask and then, just three verses later in 6:11, instructs us to pray for our daily bread? The Aramaic can clear that up.

For one thing, the style of the prayer is purely poetic. I mean with real rhyme and meter. Rabbis in ancient times did not teach from notes, all their teaching was done from memory, and the students or disciples did not take notes; they also had to memorize what their teacher was teaching. So, memory tricks were very popular. In the case of the Lord's Prayer, it was presented so that a child could easily memorize it. How many children quickly learn, "Now I lay me down to sleep, I pray the Lord my soul to keep" because it is taught as a rhyme. As a rhyme, the child easily commits it to memory. The Lord's Prayer is such a rhyme. It uses in proper metric order of words such as *hashemyem, shem lechem.*

There are also numerous word plays that are easily understood by any Aramaic-speaking child but not picked up in Greek or Latin, let alone in

English. For instance, "Our Father who is in heaven." The word heaven is *hashemyem*. It is phonetically identical to *hashama*, which means to listen. What a first-century Semite might have heard was a dual meaning. "Our Father who is in heaven" and/or "Our Father who listens." Then Jesus says: "Hallowed be thy name." The word name, *shem*, is again a play on the word hashemyem (the heavens). This is very clear in the Aramaic and not in the Greek. The word in Aramaic is more correctly translated as *the heavens* (plural with a definite article). The word "heaven" as a city we go to when we die was not a common expression in the first century. When you died, you went to the Garden of Eden, Abraham's Bosom, or as Jesus said on the Cross to the thief: "This day you will be with me in paradas (paradise)." When Jesus said: "Our Father who art in heaven," the first-century Jews immediately thought of the sky, the sun, the moon, and the stars. It was from the heavens that God sent rain and sunshine, which caused crops to grow and meet their basic need for food.

In II Chronicles 7:14:

> *If my people, which are called by my name, shall humble themselves, and pray, and seek my face, and turn from their wicked ways; then will I hear from heaven, and will forgive their sin, and will heal their land.*

We clearly have an example of the word heaven in the Hebrew as *hashamayim,* which literally means the heavens (plural) and is a direct reference not to a heavenly city but in its proper context of God ending a famine by bringing rain from the skies or the heavens.

When Jesus says: "Our Father who art in heaven (*hashemeyim*), hallowed by thy name (*shem*) there is a play on the two words. *Shem* really means reputation in Aramaic. God's reputation is one that supplies rain and sunshine to give us food and shows His faithfulness with the sun going down at night and rising in the morning. People in the first century did not know the dynamics of outer space. To them, if the gods got angry, they would blot out the sun. That is why eclipses struck such terror in the hearts of ancient man. It was taken as a warning from the gods that they had the power to blot out the sun. Yet, Jehovah never threatened to remove the sun, and it rose every morning, a daily miracle like one's daily bread.

Which brings us to the question, why do we ask the Lord for our daily bread if Jesus just got done explaining that God knows our needs before we even ask? Again, in the Aramaic, bread had a double meaning, a food source and a source of spiritual strength. Dr. Lamsa, an Aramaic scholar, explained it this way. The proper syntax is "Give us the bread of our need today." It does not say, "Give us our daily bread." This phrase has been so embedded in the Western world that we dare not question it, yet to ask God for our daily bread is showing great disrespect for His faithfulness." The word in Aramaic for give is *yahav*, which does not really mean to give but to set, place, or serve. God is handing us our bread, and we are *yahav* acknowledging our acceptance of this gift and provision by God, asking for no more or no less. Dr. Lamsa further explains: "'Give us our daily bread' does not mean that God has forgotten to supply this urgent need but that we should be satisfied with our supplies day to day."

Remember, there is a double meaning. The spiritual meaning. The word in Aramaic for war is *malechemah*; it is the word *lechem* (bread) with the preposition Mem or from and the feminine suffix Hei. All wars were fought for food and protection of one's family. Practically all ancient wars were fought for water rights and fertile land rights to grow their food and thus protect and provide for their families. God giving us our daily bread had a secondary meaning of receiving the strength we need to fight the spiritual battles of the day. I just read in the Talmud this morning in Avodah Zarah 19a to paraphrase that God has given each of us a purpose, goal, or mission in life. He has also given us the gifts and ability to accomplish this goal. I personally have not been given the purpose of leading worship in song as I have no ear for music. For the life of me, I can hear a song on the radio, and five minutes later, I am unable to hum that tune. I have yet to figure out how someone can hit a note on the piano and open their mouth and somehow get their voice to match that note. No one has yet been able to explain it to me or teach me how to accomplish this. I have spent my life trying to figure out what my purpose or goal in life and perhaps God has allowed me to exist for these many years so I could finally figure it out.

According to the Lord's prayer, "Give me this day my daily bread," I am asking God every day for the "bread" or strength and ability to accomplish the mission or goal He has placed me on this earth to fulfill.

Let's examine the portion of this prayer in Matthew 6:10: *"Thy kingdom come. Thy will be done in earth, as [it is] in heaven."* In the Aramaic, this is read as: *"May your kingdom come and your will occur as is in heaven and also on earth."* That reading doesn't change much. So let's take a look at the words that are used.

The first word to examine is *kingdom.* It seems everyone and their mother has their idea of what the kingdom is. For many, it is heaven, for some, it is the millennium, for others, it is a physical kingdom on earth where Jesus will rule, and for others, it is a spiritual kingdom, just to name a few. I do not intend to argue what it is or isn't; I only want to look at it from a Jewish point of view; that is how the Jews of the first century viewed it. So, before I share my idea of what the kingdom is, let me look at the rest of this verse, and from that, I will plug in my idea or that of the first-century Jewish idea of what the kingdom was.

Note Jesus only says kingdom, not the kingdom of heaven. Also, note that the word heaven in this verse is *dabashamyim* in Aramaic which means the heavens. As explained, the word *shamayim* or heavens was not used in the first century as our place of eternal bode. Few people listening would have thought of our eternal home after death when they heard the word *shamayim* or heaven.

The heavens is a reference to the sky, the stars, the moon, and the sun. So how is God's will done in the skies? Well, for one thing, people looked at the sky a lot, and they marveled at the orderliness of the sky, the seasons, and the rains all coming as scheduled. They stood in awe of its beauty. But they also heard something else when they heard the Aramaic word for will - *'ata. 'Ata* means one's will, desire, pleasure. Rabbi Samson Hirsch, the nineteenth-century linguist, points out that it also means beauty. In Semitic culture, the will of God always brings beauty. Say a Semitic man in the Middle East is carrying a bag of grain. The bag rips open, and all his grain is poured out on the ground. He will look up and say, "Alah wills it." This is not fatalism; it is simply a prayer that God will make something beautiful out of his tragedy.

Vincent Van Gogh, for me at least, was probably the greatest artist that ever lived. He was a very troubled man, a man suffering from deep mental depression. Yet, he took all that pain and torment and put it into color. Well, any artist can do that. Picasso did it and created something grotesque, but Van Gogh did something no artist that I am aware of could do. He took all his pain and torment, put it into color, and made something exquisitely beautiful. That is *'ata.* The will of God may sometimes be something very painful and difficult but hidden inside; He is creating something very beautiful.

"Thy kingdom come, they will be done" are jointly related, especially when viewed through the eyes of a first-century Jew. For you see, to them, the kingdom of God was the knowledge of God. The knowledge of God was the key to understanding the will or *'ata* of God, that is, the beauty found in His perfect will. To obtain the knowledge of God was to obtain the secret to understanding the pain and suffering in the world. It was the key to the miraculous; it was the key to an intimate relationship with God. Jesus even said that the Kingdom of God is found within us. An intimate relationship with God brings us into peace and security. The Kingdom of God begins now in this moment, as we live on this earth, and continues when we pass from this earth into God's presence.

The word kingdom in Aramaic is *melekavak* which comes from the root word *melek,* which means to rule, reign, deliberation, dignity. As a noun, it is used for a king, ruler, queen and kingdom. Yet, it is also a legal term, and built into every definition lies the idea of dignity and deliberation. A judge or jury will deliberate; that is, they will spend time and carefully consider all sides of an argument and then render a decision. To keep consistent with the word 'ata, we could really render this as: "Your deliberations and considerations be done, and your will create something beautiful. Then to be consistent with the "on earth as it is in the heavens" keep in mind the ancients look upon the skies and the heavenly bodies with awe at its beauty. In other words: "May the beauty and organization of the heavens be like that on earth."

We learn further in Mathew 6:13: *"And lead us not into temptation, but deliver us from evil:"* Recently, as I drove my Greek Orthodox priest friend to the dentist in my disability bus, we got to talking about the Aramaic and discussed what this passage means in Aramaic. Like so many others, we puzzled over those strange words "Lead us not into temptation."

If we quote directly from the King James Version, it sounds as if God has a tendency to lead us into temptation, and we need to specifically ask that He not do such a thing. Many people puzzle over this, and many just assume, correctly, it is just one of those things that get messed up in translation, and they figure out that what Jesus was really saying was: "Don't allow us to fall into temptation," which is really correct in the Aramaic. I am not a Greek scholar, so I cannot comment on how it should be worded from the Greek. I have found the Holy Spirit has a tendency to really cover for the ambiguity of translators, but people are still a little shaky about their understanding as that is clearly not the way it should be translated from the Greek. So they will question whether it is just their attempt to explain away a difficult passage or whether our Greek text is really accurate or not.

Even the Roman Catholic pope created quite a stir when he changed the "Our Father" to read *Do not allow me to fall into temptation.* People started to accuse the pope of changing the words of Jesus. Well, no pope in his right mind will change the words of Jesus, but what the pope did was use the Aramaic version of the prayer.

So, I do like to put people's minds at ease by assuring them that in at least one language, the language that Jesus spoke, they are right to assume the passage does not really say, *"Do not lead us into temptation."* The word used in Aramaic for *let us (not) enter* is *talan* from the root word *'al.* This is in a feminine plural jussive form in the Aramaic which implies a permissive state, *"Do not allow us to enter into temptation."*

The word for temptation is *nesiana* from the root word *nesa,* which means a trial, temptation, or a test, but according to Rabbi Hirsch, it is closely related to the word *nesas* and likely from the same root. At least it is related enough to indicate a wordplay. In other words, *nesas* is telling us just what type of trial we are talking about. *Nesas* means to be high, exalted, lifted up. Now let's keep this in context. Remember, *thy will be done* is sort of the theme of this prayer. Ultimately, that is what every prayer we make to God amounts to: "Thy will be done."

When I write my books and word studies for my blog, I pray to God: *"Thy will be done."* But, I also pray: "If your will be done and if I receive praise and honor for my writings, then don't allow me to fall into the trial or temptation of exalting myself, feeling I am better than others, lifting myself up - in a word - pride." Probably the greatest danger in doing God's will is how it opens us up to pride when the power of God and the miraculous is manifested.

I recall in seminary; we had a visiting pastor who warned us of the two most dangerous people we would find in our congregation. The first is that fellow who criticizes everything you do. You can't sneeze without him judging it, discussing its merits, and how he could do a better job at it. This person will discourage you. But an even more dangerous person is that sweet, elderly woman who will think you are the greatest preacher to ever grace the pulpit and will constantly remind you of it. The danger there is that you will believe her.

Years ago, my brother gave me a recording of a conference in the Vineyard church in Toronto, where the Toronto Blessing originated. People from all over the world came to this church to experience the Toronto Blessing. This included ministers, evangelists, teachers, etc. Of course, in the true tradition of Christianity, Pastor Arnett invited some of the celebrity and successful ministers and evangelists to the platform to give a testimony and tell of their great successes. The power of the Holy Spirit was very much manifested during this time. I know that for certainty because every time a successful or celebrity preacher got to the part of telling of his successes, he was overcome with the power of the Holy Spirit; he could not talk; he could only grunt and moan. For instance: "Oh, Yes, I spoke in a stadium filled with no less than…ugh, oh, oo, ah. Finally, he would get control of himself and continue, "…we had no less than…ugh, oh, oo, ah. The Holy Spirit was simply answering a prayer this preacher might have prayed, at least from his heart, before speaking: "Don't allow me to fall into temptation (don't let me brag about the numbers), but if I lose control of myself, and I start to brag, then deliver me from this evil."

You see, don't allow me to fall into temptation is followed by the word 'ala,' which is the word *but, rather, however, on the contrary,* or *otherwise.* In other words, the next phrase is tied into the last phrase. "Don't allow me to enter into the temptation of pride; otherwise, if I do, deliver me from this evil." Amazing that the word deliver is *petsa,* which means to rescue or save from a dangerous situation. "Don't allow me to enter into temptation of pride, but if I do, then rescue me from this evil.

The word in Aramaic that is used for *evil* is a very interesting word. It is so telling of human nature and God's understanding of human nature. It is not a *ra'* word which is the common word for evil. Rather it is the word *boshah.* Some interpret this as the evil one or satan, and I would not say they are wrong. The word has a wide range of meanings, all of which, I believe, apply to this situation. It can be as simple as a mistake or an error; it could be a difficulty or trouble, confusion, disappointment, or simply feeling ashamed of oneself. There is a common denominator in all this, and that is pride. If you think about it, most of all our troubles, confusion and disappointment stems from our pride, our pride that is wounded, challenged, or threatened.

As C.S. Lewis said in *Mere Christianity*:

> A proud man is always looking down on things and people; and, of course, as long as you are looking down, you cannot see something that is above you. As long as you are proud you cannot know God.

Finally, Matthew 6:13 concludes with: *"For thine is the kingdom and the power and the glory forever, Amen."* You will not find these words in many modern English translations. The reason for that is that many of the earlier manuscripts in the Greek do not have this conclusion. The Peshitta, the Aramaic Bible, did not either, but it was put in at a later date. Is this part of the inspired text? Did Jesus actually use these words to end the prayer? We cannot be sure, but it is a nice ending.

Actually, the Peshitta that I use has these words except the last word Amen. I already discussed the kingdom, so I will not rehash that. That leaves two key words, well, actually three if you include Amen.

I probably would not even bother with this if it wasn't for the unusual words that the Peshitta uses here. The word for power, *chayl*. That is a very unusual word for power because it is a word used for dancing and spinning around in a circle. It is also used for energy and vibrations. The word ends with an Aleph, which is a definite article in the Aramaic. God is "The Power or Vibration." Everything that exists, all matter has vibrations. When God created the world, He saw that it was good. The word good or *tov* in Hebrew means to be in harmony. When God created the world, all was in harmony with him, or all vibrated to his frequency. When man sinned that perfect harmony, that precision-tuned orchestra started hitting some sour notes. All was no longer in harmony or in frequency with Him.

God is the tuning fork for all of creation. He is The Power or the force behind everything that exists. Life and all matter have a frequency; they all vibrate. Thus, He is The Glory. I was shocked to see the word used for glory in this passage. It is the word *tishbohta*. It is not *kavod* which is both the Hebrew and Aramaic word for glory. *Tishbohta* ends with the definite article

Aleph, so He is "The Glory." It comes from the root word Shabbat. He is the Sabbath or the Rest. When you are in harmony with Him, in His frequency, you find rest. I can only find *tishbohta* in extra-Biblical literature that post-dates the time of Christ. This does not appear to be a first-century Aramaic word which would be a strong argument that this last phrase in this prayer is not in the original text. In extra-Biblical literature, I find *tshbohta* to be used as a word for *praise and song*. That would work into the word *chayl* or vibrations. For music to be in harmony, it needs to share the same frequency. I love to hear an orchestra or even a choir or a quartet singing. You have different voices or instruments, each with a different tone and sound, yet when they join in harmony, sharing the same frequency, you have beautiful, restful music. Once someone gets a little off-key, there is an annoyance; that beautiful rest is disrupted.

The final word in this prayer in many of our texts is 'amen. I explained this in an earlier chapter and will go into more detail in the final chapter.

25. KNEELING IN PRAYER

Genesis 25:11: "And it came to pass after the death of Abraham, that God blessed his son Isaac; and Isaac dwelt by the well Lahairoi."

Is there a proper bodily position we must take in prayer? The word *palal* for prayer is written with the letter Pei which represents the mouth and two Lameds. The ancient sages taught that the Lamed was a picture of a hand being lifted up to heaven. The little bump in the middle of the Lamed represents your heart. Hence the word for prayer itself shows us a picture of praying with uplifted hands, one hand reaching up to heaven with words from your heart and the other hand receiving from heaven the Words of God into your heart.

One word for praise is *halal,* which is spelled with a Hei and two Lameds. The Hei represents worship and praise, and the Lamed again pictures two hands raised in worship and praise. One hand offering to God one's worship and praise from the heart and the other hand receiving God's presence into your heart.

The word for worship is *shachah* which in its Semitic roots means to be surrounded by water as a picture of the presence of God surrounding you as you praise and worship. However, you will find that your lexicons also tell you that *shachah* also means to fall prostrate, that is, lying stretched out on the ground with one's face downward.

The Bible has numerous passages that speak of kneeling and praying as Acts 20:36: *"When he had thus spoken, he kneeled down, and prayed with them all."* Or Acts 21:5: *"And when we had accomplished those days, we departed and went our way; and they all brought us on our way, with wives and children, till we were out of the city: and we kneeled down on the shore, and prayed."*

Kneeling in prayer is something that we are all familiar with and have been raised with. This is not to mention that there is something very natural within us that causes us to fall to our knees in respect and honor.

As I approached the anniversary of my father's passing, I reflected on his graveside service. My father was a military veteran and was entitled to a military presentation of the flag of the United States. At the ceremony, the honor guard carried the folded flag to my mother, who was sitting at the graveside, and knelt down before her to present the flag. As I reflected on the ceremony, I felt a prompting to examine Genesis 25:11, where I read that God blessed Isaac, Abraham's son, after his father, Abraham, died.

You see, the word for *blessed* in Hebrew is *barak* which comes from a Semitic root *BK* and is a loan word for the Akkadian meaning *to kneel*. Every modern English translation says that God blessed Isaac. We often interpret the word bless to mean to make someone happy. In a certain context, that is true. Yet, I was reading in the Jewish Talmud in Sotah 14a that *barak* in Genesis 25:11 means to comfort. Looking at this and the Semitic root of barak, I believe a more accurate rendering of Genesis 25:11 is: "God knelt before Isaac and comforted him."

But soft, taking this word *barak* to its Semitic root creates a more beautiful picture of the nature of God's love. I was reading on the internet about the proper flag presentation protocol. It reads: "**Stand** facing the flag recipient and hold the folded flag waist high with the straight edge facing the recipient. **Lean** toward the flag recipient and solemnly present the flag to the recipient." The protocol says to "stand and lean"; it does not say to kneel. Yet when I looked at all the images on the internet of a flag presentation, most of the members of the honor guard presenting the flag are kneeling before the recipient, still holding the flag waist high (It seems the Marines always kneel–just saying). This appeared to be done as the recipient was seated. However, there were pictures where the recipient was standing, and the soldier presenting the flag was kneeling. There is nothing in the protocols that I read that requires the presenter to kneel.

I asked someone at our local VFW about this, and she said that it is the discretion of the presenter whether to kneel or not. I said the protocols instructed the presenter to stand, not kneel. The VFW representative just shrugged and said: "Who will argue such a broken protocol?" She is right; to see a highly decorated warrior in dress uniform kneel before the loved one of a deceased veteran is a very moving site and conveys a deep respect for the fallen warrior. What is even more moving is that this presenter is actually voluntarily breaking protocol by kneeling, but who would dare condemn him or her? Breaking protocol in this context shows an even greater sign of respect.

To the ancient Semitic mindset, when you say that God *barak* Isaac, the picture in their mind would be that God came to Isaac, knelt before him, and comforted him. Such a picture breaks with all the protocols we assign to God. God kneeling before us? Hey, He is God, and if He wants to break protocol to kneel before you as you grieve, who is going to condemn Him? Besides, who can convey a more loving picture than the almighty God of the universe kneeling before His grieving child to offer comfort?

That is why I render Genesis 25:11: "And it came to pass after the death of Abraham, that God knelt before his son Isaac and comforted him." Kneeling shows honor and respect, and God is not above showing such honor and respect toward us at a time when we really need it, like Isaac did when his father passed away. Kneeling before God is an act of love, and like anything else, it is meaningless if it does not come from your heart.

Kneeling before God when praying is not necessary; there are other postures to assume. But kneeling is a way to bodily express your love and respect for God. It will not prompt or motivate God to answer your prayer any quicker or with any greater certainty than if you prayed sitting or standing. It will only be a gesture from your heart to express your love and humility to God.

26. HEARING GOD'S VOICE IN PRAYER

Exodus 19:5: "Now therefore if you will obey my voice indeed and keep my commandments, Then, you will be a peculiar treasure unto me above all the people, for all the earth is mine."

Psalms 27:7 "Hear. O' Lord, when I cry with my voice; have mercy also upon me, and answer me."

"My words fly up, but my thoughts remain below." Shakespeare, <u>Hamlet</u>, Act 3, Scene 3

I recently filed an insurance claim, and after a week, I wrote to the insurance company demanding a response. Sure, I wanted to hear if they would pay the claim, but at that time, I just wanted an acknowledgment that they had received my claim. Even if they were to reject the claim, I still wanted to know if the claim was received. One frustration we seem to have with prayer is that there is no immediate acknowledgment that God has received our prayer. We are expected to just accept by faith that it was received. Does God ever really speak to us while we are praying?

In Shakespeare's play *Hamlet*, Hamlet's father, the king, had murdered his brother. Hamlet enters the king's chambers with the idea of killing the king. However, he comes upon the king while he is praying or attempting to pray and fears that if he kills the king while he is in prayer, the king will go to heaven, and he does not want that to happen. Oddly, the king is not praying that he be forgiven for his crime but that he could get away with it. His prayer is simply words and has no true meaning or feeling of remorse. The king realizes that it was a fruitless prayer and says: "My words fly up but my thoughts remain below." In other words, he knows it is a prayer that God will not hear.

Psalms 27:7 is a curious verse. David uses the word *shama* in an imperative form. The word *shama* means more than just hear; it means to listen, submit, obey, respond and become a part of, and become one with. He could have used the word *davar* or even *amar* rather than *shama*. Why does he use this particular word?

Western Christianity is very scientifically and mathematically based, whereas the Semitic culture is more poetically based. Hence, we will read this verse from the mind of a scientist and not from the heart of a poet. In other words, we make little attempt to search out the heart of the poet, to understand his torment, anguish, or his joy and his passion. Hebrew is an emotional language. You cannot just look up a word in your Lexicon and say you now know what a word means in the original Hebrew. You must take this word out for a walk, live with it, experience it, feel it, play with it, argue with it, and build a relationship with it before you really understand it. You must never translate a word just by looking it up in a lexicon, but take that word and let it simmer in your heart until you know the Spirit of God has certified it as a proper English word to use.

To use the word *shama* in an imperative form shows the depth of anguish that David is experiencing. For him to literally cry out to God to listen to him, submit to his request, obey, and become one with "his voice" shows the desperation that David feels. He wants some response from God, an assurance that God has at least heard his prayer. If you have never felt abandoned by God, never felt like your words were flying up, but your thoughts were remaining below, you will not understand the true depth of this passage. If you have had this experience or are even experiencing it now, you are in a good position to translate this verse with your heart and begin to understand the heart of David and what he was really saying in this verse.

David is asking God to obey the cry of his voice. The word cry is *qara* which is a call to meet or assemble. The word for voice is *'qoli* which has a paragogic Hei. The paragogic makes this not only a voice but a voice of anguish. David is doing more than just asking God to listen to him; he is demanding that God become a part of his anguish.

Check out Hebrew 4:15: *"For we do not have a high priest who cannot sympathize with our weakness but one who has been tempted in all things as we are, yet, without sin."* The high priest was the one who made the atonement for sin. Jesus, as our high priest, understands our weakness, the reason we so easily fall to sin, and thus when He forgives us, He also understands. He is literally saying: "I know how hard it is, I know the need that drove you to sin, I know why you sinned, I understand your anguish, and I just long to fill that need that would drive you to sin."

Do you ever feel so desperate that you are strongly tempted to do something in the flesh to ease your situation or pain? Here David is saying that God loves us so much that he is willing to share in our anguish, but not only that, He is also ready to meet whatever need it is that is causing our anguish so we do not have to resort to the arm of the flesh. In our desperation, we can actually ask God to experience that suffering with us and be a part of it. For David to use the word *shama* in an imperative form shows that God is not only willing but ready and wants to jump into the pit with us. All we have to do is what David did – ask. Perhaps next time you cry out to God to relieve your anguish, ask Him to join you in it. He wants to; he loves you so much he even wants to share in your anguish and walk you through it without sin. Like Benjamin Franklin said: "He who is in the mud, likes to pull another in." Jesus is there with His hand out, offering to jump in the fray with you. If the storms of life toss you overboard, Jesus will not only long to be with you in that water, but He will be willing to jump overboard and tread water with you.

But note this verse: Exodus 19:5: *"Now therefore if you will obey my voice indeed and keep my commandments, Then you will be a peculiar treasure unto me above all the people, for all the earth is mine."* What catches my attention in this verse is the thought that God loves us, He loves everybody, but there are apparently those who He not only loves, but He treasures.

With that thought, let's take a closer look at this verse. We become this treasure if we obey His voice. That is really tricky. If you actually heard God's voice and knew without a doubt it was God's voice, would you really do anything else but obey? I hear people all the time saying: "Well, God spoke to me and said...." "God told me the other day...." Hey, I even say it. But like most people, most Christians for that matter, I do have a bit of hesitation. Was it really God's voice I heard? I mean, if I felt a strong impression to throw $10.00 in an offering plate, well, I would do it, just to be on the safe side of obeying what I felt was God's voice. But if I felt a strong impression to stand on a street corner and begin to preach, I think I would need more than a strong impression. Even if I heard an actual voice, I would most likely question my sanity before doing something insane, like standing on a street corner and preaching. But if I knew beyond any doubt God asked me to do it, I would not hesitate, and I daresay neither would you. It is not a matter of desire to obey God but just an assurance that you really heard from God. I am sure Noah did not hesitate to spend his next hundred years building an ark, but he sure must have had some pretty definite confirmation he actually heard God's voice.

The word for voice is *qaval* which is *speaking, calling, voice,* etc., but it is also used for *nonverbal communication as well.* Three elements make up the word for voice in *qaval.* The first letter Qop represents God speaking through a natural or human instrument like a preacher or teacher. The second letter Vav is God speaking through an inward connection, that strong impulse, impression, or feeling. The last letter, Lamed, is God speaking through the Word of God, the Bible.

Rabbi Samson Hirsch gives one definition of *qaval* as an outward expression of one's thoughts. It is closely associated with the word *qalah or restraining* and *qalal to diminish.* I believe what Rabbi Hirsch is saying is that as we restrain our wants and desires and as we diminish our outward concerns, the voice of God becomes clearer.

I remember when I was living in silence before God a couple of years ago. It was like my third or fourth day of silence, of living in the presence of God 24/7 and spending each day diminishing my personal desires and restraining my impulses, that I really began to hear God's *qaval.* It was not audible, but I heard it all around me, in Scripture, in my thoughts, and even as I walked among His creation. I heard a woodpecker tapping away at a tree. I felt this inward urging to listen to the tapping. As a child, I was interested in Morse code. By the third or fourth day, I thought it not strange to consider that God might be sending me a message through this woodpecker. I know some would say it was just my imagination, and after three days in silence, I probably really believed God's *qaval* was in that woodpecker's tapping, and my desire for it to be so made it so. But I know deep within my own heart it was a message from God .. .-.. ..- ...- -.-- --- .-.- *I luv you.* God has many ways of speaking to us, and when you diminish yourself and restrain your impulses, you will hear His *qaval* in more ways than you can imagine.

27. AMEN

Genesis 15:6: "And he (Abraham) believed the Lord and He counted it as righteousness."

What better way to conclude a book on prayer than to end it with the word Amen. I know I shared a little about this earlier in the book, but I just want to sum it up.

The Talmud teaches that *trusting belief* in God is more important than anything else. One may keep all the laws of Torah and follow every ritual, but it is only trust that will ultimately save the individual. Remember how Saul lost his kingdom because he performed a sacrifice before a battle rather than wait for Samuel to arrive to do it? Samuel was late, and Saul's army was deserting him, but Saul would not go to war until that sacrifice was offered, so he did it himself. What was his sin? Yes, disobedience, of course. But I never heard a Christian preacher or teacher give the root reason. I had to go to Jewish literature to find it. It was that Saul was not trusting or believing in God. It is ironic that we, as Christians who know and understand that our salvation is in faith in God alone and not works, will not see this, yet the Jews, whom we say depend upon works, are the ones who do recognize faith as their cornerstone, go figure.

The Talmud teaches that if a drowning man suddenly spots a tree within reach, which part of the tree does he lunge for? Not the branches, for they will break under his weight; rather, he grabs the roots of the tree. Trusting in God is similar to the strong roots of a tree; it is the basis and foundation of the entire tree, our salvation.

The word in Genesis 15:6 for *believe* is *amen*. When you trace this word to its Semitic roots, you find that it has its origins in the nursing of a baby. Consider the dynamics involved in a nursing baby. The mother must cradle the baby in her arms. The baby is in total protection of its mother. The mother is providing sustenance to the baby directly from herself, not from a spoon or cup, and it is her own milk, not the milk of a goat or cow. The impressionist artist Mary Cassatt in her famous painting "Louise Nursing Her Child," depicts a mother nursing her child with the mother looking at her baby with total love in her eyes and the baby looking up to its mother with total trust and dependence in its eyes. That painting could easily have been named *Amen*. Mary Cassatt spoke volumes in this painting, portraying the deep bonding taking place between the mother and child. This is why I use the word *trust* for *amen* rather than belief, although our English word *belief* does fit *amen*.

As a man watches his wife nurse their baby, he sees a picture, one like that beautifully portrayed by Mary Cassatt; she is fulfilling her role as a helpmeet for she is giving this man a visual demonstration of belief, amen. From this, he can begin to understand what *amen (trust, belief)* in God really means. Yet, a man cannot understand the full meaning of *amen*, at least not like a woman, for he cannot feel or experience *amen* like a woman. That is why it is so important for a woman to learn to love her husband like she automatically loves her child so she can be an *'ezer kenegedo helpmeet* to her husband.

I remember hearing the wife of a veteran who was badly burned in combat. His face was totally disfigured, and he refused to believe that his wife could still love him. The wife said she had to learn to love him as she would a child before it was born, and then as she nursed him back to health, this veteran began to realize that he had to learn to believe that his wife really loved him before he could fully recover.

It is interesting that the Bible uses the words *'ezer kenegedo helper who stands before him* for the word *helpmeet*. The enemy knows how dangerous a woman is to his cause. Through the granting of the ability to bring life into this world and experience the intimacy of nursing that new life, she has been given knowledge of the love of God and the duty to pass that knowledge unto a man. No wonder the enemy is creating pornography, homosexuality, and destroying the home. Therein lays the very core of understanding the love of God. Is it any wonder that the enemy wants to promote the male as in a dominant role rather than just a leadership role? He has to keep the woman underfoot lest she reveal the true nature of the love of God to her husband. It was never intended by God for a woman to be dominated by her husband; he was only to be a leader. The woman was created to *ezer kenegedo*, to stand before the man and be a gateway to the knowledge of God's love.

That is why Solomon said in Proverbs 18:22 that whosoever finds a wife finds a *good (tov)* thing. I hate the word *thing; obviously* a male translation. I like the Living Bible's rendering; "Whosoever finds a wife finds a treasure." The word *tov* means to bring into harmony; thus, whosoever finds a wife finds someone who can bring him into *tov perfect harmony* with God.

The word amen in Judaism is a very commonly used word and is recognized as appearing throughout the Torah. The Talmud in Shavuot 36a teaches that there are three intentions within the word amen, and it depends upon the context in which of the three you use.

The first would be as an oath, as we find in *Numbers 5:22 "And this water that causeth the curse shall go into thy bowels, to make thy belly to swell, and thy thigh to rot: And the woman shall say, Amen, amen."* When the Sanhedrin would administer an oath, the person would answer with "Amen," upon which it would be considered as if they themselves had sworn.

Secondly, it would show an acceptance of a statement. During a midrash, after a matter has been discussed and debated, all present had to *amen* their conclusion. If just one did not *amen* the conclusion, the final statement would be rejected.

Thirdly, it would be used for confirmation of (or faithfulness in) a statement. When a person would testify as to the work that the Lord accomplished or would accomplish, it would be followed by all who believed it to be true with *amen*. This would include the expression of a belief, a prayer, or in any statement that one would anticipate a fulfillment.

As you can see, the word *amen* is versatile and is used to respond to many things, from blessings, prayers to praise of God as well as after reciting and/ or hearing prayers of request or supplication to God. *Amen* signifies an affirmation of belief. The letters of the word *amen* are the same root letters for the word *emunah,* which means to believe or trust.

The Talmud in Beracht 53b teaches us that the person who responds amen to a blessing, testimony, or prayer is even greater than the one who is saying the blessing, testimony, or prayer. So, keep that in mind the next time your pastor says something that you wish to affirm.

The Talmud in Shabbat 119b adds something very interesting in the use of the word *amen*. It is taught that: "one should be careful to prolong the word (*amen*) for the length of time it takes to say the words *El Melech ne'eman* (God is a faithful king). For ultimately, this is the meaning of the term *amen,* which is an acronym for the Hebrew words *El Melech ne'eman* (God is a faithful king."

So with that, may I conclude this study by saying: AAAAAAAAAMEN! GOD IS FAITHFUL!

ABOUT THE AUTHOR

Chaim Bentorah is the pseudonym of a Gentile Christian who taught college-level Biblical Hebrew and is an Amazon Bestselling Author. He prepared his students to take the placement exams for graduate school. He has now developed a method of study where he can prepare any Believer, regardless of age or academic background, to study the Word of God using Biblical Hebrew.

Chaim Bentorah received his B.A. degree from Moody Bible Institute in Jewish Studies and his M.A. degree from Denver Seminary in Old Testament and Hebrew and his PhD in Biblical Archeology. His Doctoral Dissertation was on the "Esoteric Structure of the Hebrew Alphabet." He has taught Classical Hebrew at World Harvest Bible College for thirteen years and also taught Hebrew for three years as a language course for Christian Center High School. He is presently teaching Biblical Hebrew and Greek to pastors in the Metro Chicago area.

www.chaimbentorah.com

OTHER BOOKS BY CHAIM BENTORAH

- Aramaic Word Study II: Discover God's Heart In The Language Of The New Testament
- Swimming In His Presence: A Hebrew Teacher Reflects On Worship and Praise
- Aramaic Word Study: Exploring The Language Of The New Testament
- Stargates, Time Travel, And Alternate Universes
- Time Loop: Seeing America's Future in Persia's Past
- Hebrew Word Study: Exploring The Mind Of God
- Ten Words That Will Change Everything You Know About God
- Does The Bible Really Sat That?
- Treasures of the Deep
- Learning God's Love Language
- Learning God's Love Language Workbook
- Hebrew Word Study: Revealing The Heart Of God
- Journey into Silence
- Whom My Soul Loves
- Intimacy With God
- Is This Really Revival?
- Biblical Truths From Uncle Otto's Farm

CHAIM BENTORAH
ALL-ACCESS LEARNING CHANNEL

www.hebrewwordstudy.com

The Jewish poet, Hayim Nahman Bialik, once said that to study the Holy Scriptures in any language other than the original Hebrew is like kissing a beautiful woman with a veil between your face and hers.

You see, not only are all the words themselves inspired by God but their very design and nature are inspired by God are as well. God created each Hebrew word with a purpose and beauty. As there is an intelligent design in all of God's creation, so too is there an intelligent design in the language of the Old Testament, the Biblical Hebrew. **On our All-Access membership channel**, we reveal the depths of God's design in this language, revealing its beauty and understanding with the goal of creating an intimate relationship with God through His Written word.

You will discover that the Hebrew language is a masterpiece of God used to communicate His love, nature, character, and longing for humankind. There is no other language that condenses so much in so little space. It is truly the best language to deliver the living Word of God. The Jews refer to it as the Sea of Torah. It is believed that almost 80% of the oceans remain unexplored. So too, I believe we have only begun to peer into the depths of God's Word. It is impossible to explore the depths of the ocean of Scripture in just one English translation of the Bible. To really explore its depths, one needs to really understand the nature of the original language itself. For instance, our English translation may translate a word as "because." Yet there are many other possible English renderings, such as the word "heel." In our weekly Torah Portion Study, we recently addressed this word, and rather than follow the traditional rendering as "because," we discussed the possibilities of the use of the word "heel," as suggested by ancient rabbis. Suddenly, this one change in the English word from "because" to "heel" took us to the depths of the ocean of God's Word to reveal something of beauty that the English translations could never express.

We also explore the rich meanings that are found in words that are commonly overlooked, such as numbers, names, locations, colors, plant species, and animal species. We never say that our translations are wrong or mistranslated. On the contrary, it is a translator's greatest frustration that they cannot convey the depth and beauty of a Hebrew word as a translator is restricted to only one or two English words. It is like trying to describe a beautiful sunset in only one word.

My study and ministry partner described her very first class in Biblical Hebrew (similar to the Hebrew 101 class on our All-Access channel). She told how she was filled with excitement as her mind was trying to keep up with her spirit. She could see God's fingerprint and design in the language leading her to a treasure of discovery that would result in an intimate relationship with God. It was like she had been viewing the Scriptures in black and white and then suddenly seeing Scripture open up into beautiful technicolor. It was like taking a passage of Scripture as you would take a drop of water and put it under a microscope. To the naked eye, you might see a drop of water, maybe a little cloudy, but when under the microscope, you visit a new world that you never knew existed. A world filled with life and activity. So too, with studying the Scripture in the original languages. All you see is a drop of water, maybe a little cloudy, but when you study in the Biblical languages, you discover a world you never knew existed, a world teaming with spiritual life and spiritual activity.

You could also compare it to looking at a painting in a museum. You can examine its color, lines, shapes, and style. This is what one does when one studies the Word of God in one language. But when you study the Bible in the original language, it is like stepping into that painting and becoming a part of the living, moving, active scene.

After a few years of studying together, my study partner suggested we become ministry partners as we could not keep this information ourselves. We believed we were not alone in our longing to discover the depths of God's living word, and we needed to find some way to share this information with those who had the same cry of their spirits to experience the beauty of God's

Word through the original languages of Greek, Hebrew, and Aramaic. We opened a blog and began to share our Hebrew and Aramaic word studies on this blog. We also published a number of books, and from that, our publisher encouraged and helped us open a membership channel for those who were serious about their study of God's Word. On this channel, we guide our members in the use of all the online resources that give the average believer who never had the chance to attend a Bible college or seminary the ability to study the Word of God like a seminary graduate.

This All-Access channel has created a community of like-minded believers throughout the world who come together to study the Word of God, not only in light of its original languages but also from depths of Jewish literature written by sages, Jewish teachers, and rabbis over the last three thousand years.

The Jews are the people of the Old Testament, the guardians of the Hebrew language, and the chosen people of God to bring and demonstrate the knowledge and truth of the one God, the creator of all things.

This All-Access channel is run by myself and my study partner. My study partner also has been in ministry for over 30 years, helping believers to grow in their relationship with God and into an intimacy with Him. I have studied the Word of God in the original Hebrew, Aramaic, and Greek for a minimum of 3-4 hours a day for the last 45 years. I have also studied the works of rabbinical literature for over 40 years which include the Talmud, Midrash, and Targum.

There are many different ways to study Hebrew. You can study in an academic institution. You can learn to speak the modern language known as Israeli. Or you can learn the way I teach Hebrew, learning it for the sole purpose of studying the Word of God. Learning Hebrew this way is the easiest and quickest. There is no need for memorizing complex rules of grammar. A short Hebrew course is offered on All-Access, which you can take if you wish, but it is not required. I teach a live weekly Torah study on the Jewish Sabbath each week, and on Monday evening, I conduct a Hebrew/Aramaic workshop where we apply many rules of grammar. You do not need to take the Hebrew or Aramaic course to attend this class, and you may really find it to be an easier way to learn to use Biblical Hebrew as we take a hands-on approach. My study partner also teaches word-by-word Bible studies over passages of Scripture like the Song of Solomon and the Psalms.

Made in United States
Orlando, FL
27 April 2024

46231775R00098